URBAN DESIGN AS PUBLIC POLICY

JONATHAN BARNETT

URBAN DESIGN AS PUBLIC POLICY

PRACTICAL METHODS FOR IMPROVING CITIES

FOREWORD BY JOHN V. LINDSAY

ARCHITECTURAL RECORD BOOKS

Editor: Jeanne M. Davern

Graphic Designer: Jan V. White

Project Manager: Hugh S. Donlan

Production Supervisor: Susanne LanFranchi

Typography by: University Graphics, Inc.

Printed by: Halliday Lithograph Corporation

Bound by: The Maple Press Company

Published by Architectural Record,
a McGraw-Hill Publication,
1221 Avenue of the Americas,
New York, New York 10020.

Library of Congress Cataloging in Publication Data.
Barnett, Jonathan.
   Urban design as public policy.

   1. Cities and towns—Planning—United States.
I. Title.
HT166.B375   309.2′62′0973   73-88222
ISBN 0–07–003766–3

Contents

Foreword

We are fast becoming a nation of cities, indeed a world of cities, and their problems and promise must occupy the forefront of national concern. New York is a city that is both unique and prototypical: we know with pride and exasperation that there is no place like it; we also feel that it somehow embodies all the problems, and all the opportunities, of cities everywhere.

When I became Mayor of New York City, I tried to attract and retain city employees who possessed the traditional virtues of the public servant, but were able to face unprecedented problems, treat them as opportunities, and devise new and effective solutions.

I feel fortunate that among the people I was able to bring into public life were architects like Jon Barnett, Jaque Robertson, Richard Weinstein, and Alex Cooper. They formed the nucleus of a pioneering Urban Design Group which we created to bring new stature, coherence and boldness to our city's urban planning.

They were able to do exactly what was needed: think about old problems in new ways, and help redirect the city's energies accordingly.

In the process, I think they became fundamentally different people than they would have been if they had remained within the confines of the architectural profession. Instead of being architects who design buildings, they have become urban designers who can use their design skills in a variety of situations. They can work with politicians, developers, and community groups; they understand the forces that shape the city, and they have learned how to turn them in new and better directions. They have emerged from the crucible of the city as a new kind of professional, and have enlarged the capabilities of city government as a result.

I am enormously proud that people have come from all over the country, in fact from all over the world, to see our urban design accomplishments in New York. They come to study our incentive zoning legislation, our special design districts, and the new ways we have found to save landmark buildings and rebuild theaters and shopping streets. They are watching with interest our attempts to create objective standards for housing quality and planned unit development, and our methods of involving communities in the design and planning of all aspects of the city — from housing to highways and from new streetlights to new towns in the heart of town — as New York constantly rebuilds and revitalizes itself.

Jon Barnett provides a readable and well organized description of all these efforts, and more, in this book, along with the theoretical context that holds this work together. His account of our experience stands as a record of accomplishment for our own city, and gives us an opportunity to learn from our successes —and from our mistakes as well.

I believe that this description of our efforts in New York will help other cities to study our urban design techniques, and adapt our more successful efforts to their own needs. I also hope that this book will educate politicians to the importance of urban design, while stimulating other young architects and planners to enter government and carry forward this tradition.

JOHN V. LINDSAY

Introduction

City design as a real-life problem

The problems of our cities, the countryside and the environment in general are painfully evident; and, had you been lucky enough not to notice, you could hardly have missed the flood of television documentaries or newspaper and magazine articles describing them.

There is some danger that all of this mobilization of public opinion will be self-defeating in the end. After all, it is a rare person these days who is actually in favor of slum housing, or enjoys breathing polluted air. After a while, however, if people find that they can't do anything about a subject, they will stop wanting to hear it discussed. It would be unfortunate if "the urban crisis" and "the environment" joined the threat of atomic warfare in being considered situations that we will just have to learn to live with.

There is no escape from these problems. The traditional lines of demarcation between city and suburb, or between rural and urban areas, have been obliterated by the process of growth and change that has taken place in the last few decades.

The damaging side effects of this growth and change have brought a new public understanding of ecology, and the relatedness of the actions we take that affect the environment. What is not so well understood is that this relatedness is characteristic of man-made actions as well. Interstate highways designed to connect existing cities create new patterns of growth. Paying farmers not to plant crops sends large numbers of rural farm workers to the cities. Making mortgage money readily available for houses causes cities to spread and cuts down the construction of apartments. An evolving methodology for anticipating the consequences of urban growth and change, and turning them to positive effect, is the subject of this book.

We start with the assumption that we can not afford to write off our cities . . .

This book assumes that there is public acceptance of the need for dealing with urban and environmental problems if ways can be found to do so. It is not concerned with setting forth the serious failures and inequities of our society, assuming that the author and the reader deplore them equally, nor does it pretend to present answers to the full range of issues confronting us. Instead, we will be concerned with techniques for dealing with a number of significant urban and environmental problems which are found in exist-

2

ing cities, or are created when new areas are developed. The working methods shown are specific and practicable. In most cases they are accompanied by executed examples, so that the reader can decide for himself whether they represent an improvement over existing conditions and methods.

We start with the assumption that we can not afford to write off the very substantial investment, social, financial, and cultural, in the existing fabric of our cities. Perhaps this seems an obvious and unnecessary assertion; but most of the widely publicized concepts about designing cities start from the opposite premise.

What is called the "Modern Movement" in architecture has tended to advocate wiping out existing cities and replacing them with something more rational and hygienic. The French-Swiss architect, Le Corbusier, in his famous Voisin Plan for obliterating Paris, produced what is perhaps the most widely remembered image of modern town planning. Only Notre Dame and a few other historic buildings would have survived. The

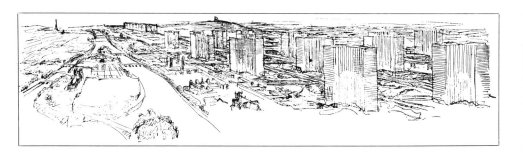

studies of the Congress International de l'Architecture Moderne (C.I.A.M.) had a rather similar intent.

Le Corbusier's Voisin Plan for Paris: writing off the city and starting over again.

These polemics against existing cities have been very influential in ways that their authors did not foresee. What began as a romantic vision of modern technology freeing the individual from the constraints of tradition has turned out to be admirably suited to mindless bureaucratic repetition, and the cost-cutting of profit-minded entrepreneurs.

The inhumane environment and stereotyped design that critics like Jane Jacobs have so justly criticized in the average urban renewal project are a direct consequence of this "modernist" concept of the city.

The modern city, and the modern social organization of which it is a part, are clearly far more subtle and complex than the revolutionary vision of fifty years ago had recognized.

Unfortunately, architects and planners have too often reacted to the evident failure of their theories about cities not by revising their theories, but by condemning society, and by indulging in escapist fantasies.

It is amazing how many texts on urban design confine themselves to the questions that concerned city designers in the eighteenth century: the enclosure of plazas and streets, the axis, the vista, the progression. These issues are important, and it is true that the "modernists" very foolishly ignored them; but there are many design problems in today's cities where these traditional concepts are not much help.

Another form of escapism is a rush to embrace a future where everything will be mechanized, and communication will be both instantaneous and total. Designers have spent their time portraying cities as walking pods, spherical honeycombs, or endlessly spreading "space frames." Aside from the fact that such proposals ignore our existing inventory of cities, the social structure necessary to make such futuristic visions work would be the most regressive imaginable.

The most subtle form of escape is to say that cities are the expression of the society that cre-

. . . nor can we afford to indulge in escapist fantasies

These two drawings are repeatedly published in architectural books and magazines: Ron Herron's *Walking City,* and Paolo Soleri's *Babel 2c.* Not only are these visions unrelated to our society, but surely no one would wish to live under the regimented conditions such cities would require.

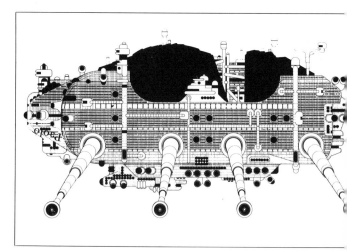

ated them, and there is no hope for cities until society is reformed.

Certainly no one who has lived in the slums of our cities, or has talked to and worked with the people who live in them, can have much satisfaction about the way our society works today. Each designer must decide how he will respond to this situation, but making physical improvements in cities is a process intimately connected to the social and power structures, and it is in the area of physical conservation or change that people trained as designers are most likely to have a useful contribution to make.

Today's city is not an accident. Its form is usually unintentional, but it is not accidental. It is the product of decisions made for single, separate purposes, whose interrelationships and side effects have not been fully considered. The design of cities has been determined by engineers, surveyors, lawyers, and investors each making individual rational decisions for rational reasons, but leaving the design of the city to be taken care of later, if at all.

Cities are created by a continuous decision-making process

Cities are not designed by making pictures of the way they should look twenty years from now. They are created by a decision-making process that goes on continuously, day after day. If people trained as designers are to influence the shape of the city, they must be present when the critical design decisions are being made.

While people of importance in government and real estate are used to considering "design" as the icing on the cake, the design professional is also to blame for his lack of influence over the form of cities.

Architects and planners have inherited some funny ideas about themselves as the keepers of the sacred flame of culture and the guardians of society's conscience. There has been a tradition that a true professional, and, certainly, a true artist, should not be too closely involved in the day-to-day process of government, or politics, or real estate development. Instead, he has sent his instructions to the policy makers as manifestos or visionary drawings, and, not surprisingly, the policy makers usually find them impossibly idealistic and irrelevant to the problem at hand.

The day-to-day decisions about the allocation of government money according to conflicting needs and different political interests, or the economics of real-estate investment, are in fact the medium of city design, as essential to the art as paint to the painter. To produce meaningful results, from both a practical and artistic point of view, urban designers must rid themselves of the notion that their work will be contaminated by an understanding of political and real estate decisions. It is not always necessary to approve; it is essential to understand.

The process of making an urban design concept politically viable or economically feasible may give an unexpected, but valuable, assist to the design process itself. It may even change the nature of the design objectives. In the words of the Cunard slogan, "getting there is half the fun," and who can be sure of a destination that is fifteen or twenty years away?

Instead of handing over city designs as an ostensibly finished product, from a position outside the decision-making process, designers of cities should seek to write the rules for the significant choices that shape the city, within an institutional framework that can be modified as times, and needs, change.

When John Lindsay became Mayor of New York City in 1966, he instituted a process that permitted designers to participate in important decisions about the future of the City. Some of the results of this experiment form the contents of this book.

It is by participating in these day-to-day decisions that designers can make a useful contribution to the future of the city

6

While many of the City's problems can not be cured by improvements in urban design, the issues involved are not trivial. Urban design can make a substantial difference to the welfare and livelihood of large segments of the population. In fact, little in the way of urban design would have been achieved in New York if community groups and trade unions, small businessmen and large financial institutions, had not perceived that various urban design proposals were very much in their interest.

As I took part in this major effort to change the way that New York City is designed, I can not be objective about the significance of what happened. I believe, however, that what was done in New York should prove applicable in many other contexts; and, while some aspects of our experience do have their parallels in other cities, the commitment to urban design on the part of the City administration has not been matched elsewhere in the country.

Perhaps a few words are in order describing how we happened to be in the right place at the right moment in time.

How the author and his colleagues came to take part in the design of New York City

By 1965, when John V. Lindsay decided to run for Mayor of New York City, I and two other architects, Jaquelin Robertson and Richard Weinstein, had spent many long lunches talking about possible ways to influence the important design decisions about cities. The Lindsay campaign looked to be an opportunity to put some of our ideas to work. Two like-minded architects, Giovanni Pasanella and Myles Weintraub, joined us, and together we went down to campaign headquarters and offered our services.

Fortunately, the man who met with us was Donald Elliott, who was an important figure in the campaign and had the imagination to try us out and see if we came up to our own valuation (as we were then in our late twenties or early thirties, there was little evidence for Donald to go on.) He put us to work developing position papers on planning and design, particularly in the area of community participation and the decentralization of city government.

After Lindsay was elected, Donald became the co-ordinator of the transitional period before the Mayor took office, and then became Counsel to the

Mayor. We were appointed to a study group on decentralization of the Mayor's office, and later became consultants for a prototype community planning study in the East Tremont neighborhood of the Bronx.

Meanwhile, the Mayor had established a task force on urban design, headed by CBS Board Chairman William S. Paley. Jaque Robertson was one of the members of this group. The report of the Paley study recommended that the City should establish a permanent capacity for dealing with urban design questions, which had traditionally been answered by consulting studies when they were considered at all. The best place for such a group, the Paley report stated, would be the staff of the City Planning Commission.

Not entirely coincidentally, Donald Elliott had by this time become Chairman of the City Planning Commission; and he argued persuasively that we should put aside our ideas of starting a private practice and establish the Planning Commission's Urban Design Group. Giovanni Pasanella had too many professional commitments to be able to do this, but the rest of us went to work for the City in April of 1967.

In the beginning, we ran the Urban Design Group without a formal hierarchy, rather on the model of an architectural partnership. The Mayor, who was amused by our efforts to avoid being traditional bureaucrats, introduced each of us, at one time or another, as the director of the Urban Design Group. Later, as the numbers of urban designers working for the City grew, and their jobs became more complicated, a more formal assignment of responsibilities became necessary.

Jaquelin Robertson and Richard Weinstein moved over to the Mayor's office, Jaque to direct a newly created Office of Midtown Planning and Development and Richard to head the Office of Lower Manhattan Development. I remained at the Planning Commission to run the Design Group. Myles Weintraub, who had decided to go back into private practice in partnership with an eminent architect, continued to advise the City on a number of important matters on a consulting basis.

The Paley task force had expected, and so had we, that all urban design issues before the City government could be dealt with by a centralized office; but the nature of city government is such that most decision-makers will only take advice from people who work for them, or, if the advice takes the form of an order, from the Mayor. Consequently a different pattern emerged, in which urban designers were used to staff special development offices with the authority of the Mayor behind them, and were also dispersed throughout the Planning Commission and other City agencies, such as the Housing and Development Administration and the Transportation Administration.

The Urban Design Group became an initiator of special projects and a work force for design issues that involve the co-ordination of many different agencies. The director of the Design Group also represents the Mayor on the Art Commission, which must approve the design of all City-funded buildings, and serves as staff director for the Mayor's Council on Urban Design.

It was necessary to draw up a number of civil service titles for urban designers, for which exams could be held in proper form. Ultimately, a special graduate program was created at the City College, to insure the supply of qualified urban designers, a program that I now direct. There is reason to hope that urban design has become an accepted part of the New York City government, and will survive the transition to another administration.

Establishing the urban design function in the City government, however, required the active and continuing encouragement of Mayor Lindsay and Donald Elliott. Without the Mayor's firm support and Donald's advocacy, we would have lost out over several critical issues, whose favorable resolution established the credibility of our efforts. The intervention of the Mayor's Council on Urban Design also proved decisive on several occasions, and there has been much valuable support from professional and civic organizations.

Urban design can succeed if it has the support of the decision-makers

In the end, anything accomplished by city government is very much a group effort, and large numbers of people, from Commissioners to draftsmen, have been involved in the various urban design efforts described in the following pages, as have many private practitioners and consultants. Many of them are mentioned in subsequent chapters, and a more complete list of credits, on a project by project basis, can be found on page 194.

The following chapters are organized around seven major areas of concern. The first is the concept of safeguarding the public's interest in privately financed real estate development, as illustrated by the special Theater Zoning District, which was the first example of this principle we encountered. The next chapter describes further applications and more detailed experiences with special zoning districts and design review, and shows how these methods can be used to design large areas of the city without designing the buildings.

The special problems of preserving landmarks and other links to the past are the subject of the third chapter.

Chapter four, neighborhood planning and community participation, describes ways in which urban design, with the assistance of members of the public, can be used to preserve urban neighborhoods and solve some of the problems connected with living in the city.

Chapter five describes the usefulness of urban design, in the present fragmented state of our metropolitan areas, in helping existing city centers compete with suburbs and new cities.

In chapter six, highways and rapid transit systems are identified as primary determinants of city design today, and ways of controlling and using these powerful elements are described.

Finally there is a discussion of methods of conducting design review studies and insuring environmental quality, and the book concludes with some observations about urban design as a new professional discipline.

Again, no claims are advanced that urban design is a cure-all. It ought to be self-evident, but somehow is not, that cities can not solve their problems without the aid of national housing, employment, welfare and education policies. Otherwise, those cities that are doing relatively well will simply become a magnet to people from places which are not; and all the gains will be lost.

Nevertheless, it is still sound policy to do what we can. The answers to many problems lie at the end of a winding road. If you do not set out, you will never arrive.

1

Private enterprise and public benefit

Most of our cities and suburbs have been constructed by private investors. While the government builds or participates in the financing of an increasing number of structures, it seems likely that the majority of the buildings we see around us will continue to be initiated by private enterprise for a long time to come.

Real-estate developers have one overwhelmingly obvious objective . . .

Real estate developers have one overwhelmingly obvious objective: they want to make money; and, as they are in a high-risk business, they want to make a great deal of money. Some people who are concerned about the future of the environment feel that it is wrong that the guiding principle of development should be the profit motive; and even the real estate investor himself is likely to agree that private enterprise has generally not been successful in creating satisfactory cities, or in conserving the natural landscape.

To understand the limitations of real estate development you should think of it as proceeding according to a set of rules which are essentially similar to those governing the game of "Monopoly." You probably remember that the Monopoly board is marked off into squares, most of which are named after places in Atlantic City, New Jersey: Oriental Avenue, Marvin Gardens, Boardwalk. Players throw dice to move around the board. If you land on a street that no other player owns (and you have enough money), you can buy it; and having assembled all the streets in the same color group you can improve them with "houses" and "hotels," charging more and more exploitive rents to other players who land on your property.

The surveyor has marked off most of our cities and towns into a real-life Monopoly board of lots; and, even in the most rural areas, the invisible but unyielding lines of property have been superimposed on the natural landscape.

When you look down on a landscape from an airplane, the underlying game board is revealed most clearly. Here stands a new, raw street with houses under construction; next door is an old-fashioned estate with its lawns and woods intact; then more new houses, next a farm still in cultivation, a highway interchange with a small shopping center and a motel near by, then more houses, and another farm, and so on. The pursuit of profit is what shapes our environment.

The developer of the houses or the shopping center, like the Monopoly player, had first to assemble enough lots that had not been "improved" to their full economic potential so that he could build the new development he had in mind. He probably went about this as secretly as possible, because, if other players of the real-estate game had found out what he was up to, they might have moved to block his assemblage, or the owners of the properties would have held out for a higher price.

Often the location of a new development is determined by ease of assemblage as much as by more logical land use factors. An old lady's attachment to the estate her father built, or a young farmer's determination to stick to the land in the face of tempting offers and rising property taxes, deflect the entrepeneur to other properties more easily developed. The result is the familiar urban sprawl, where the old pattern is lost, and no satisfactory new pattern is created.

If your aim were to create a situation where cities are to be developed in a coherent fashion, you would not use the game of "real estate" as it is presently played. Nothing is more damaging to coherence and planning than the creation of a large number of arbitrarily shaped lots, with ownership divided among thousands of individuals.

. . . which is not always compatible with the coherent development of the city

Similarly, if you wished to conserve the natural landscape, and give new settlements a compact and coherent form, you would not mark the land off along arbitrary geometric lines, and let use and function fall where they may.

The secrecy required for land assemblage is another factor that makes coherence and planning difficult to achieve, and the competitive nature of the game creates unnecessary duplication, fragmenting the urban pattern even more.

There are established alternatives to land development based on profit. For example, the City of Stockholm purchased most of the land surrounding it in the early part of this century, and has thus been able to exercise total control over its development and growth. Great Britain, in the Town and Country Planning Act of 1947, moved to, in effect, nationalize the land, as have the socialist countries.

While private development has its limitations, development through government control is also far from perfect. If private real-estate entrepreneurs produce too fragmentary and wasteful a result, development controlled by governmental agencies can be slow and cumbersome, and its product unimaginative and stereotyped. The bureaucratic system does not seem as successful as the market place in providing for a wide range of human desires and experiences.

In any event, large-scale government spending for land acquisition, or as compensation for land nationalization, doesn't seem likely to happen in the United States in the immediate future. In the meantime, the game of real estate goes on, and some method needs to be found to direct and improve it.

An instructive conflict with a real-estate developer

Soon after we joined the staff of the Planning Commission, we found ourselves in a conflict with a real-estate developer who taught us some valuable lessons about safeguarding the public's interest in private development.

A large development firm, Sam Minskoff and Sons, had purchased the old Astor Hotel, on the west side of Times Square between 43rd and 44th Streets. Most of this property was zoned C-6-4, a high-intensity commercial district.

Several years previously, the Planning Commission had made some adjustments to the zoning district boundary, and the developer felt that he had reached an understanding with the Commission that, in due course, a special permit would be issued that would permit him some infraction of the "sky exposure plane." This action would allow the developer to build a straight tower, without setbacks, that had larger floor sizes than the tower he could build "by right."

The developer had concluded arrangements to tear down the hotel, and told his architects to proceed with the construction drawings of the building that he intended to call One Astor Plaza.

In the meantime, however, the City had acquired a new Mayor, the Planning Commission had a new Chairman, and a troop of intrepid urban designers—my colleagues and I—had arrived on the scene. The developers were dismayed to learn that the Planning Commission was disposed to consider their special permit as a new issue.

I wish I could say that we all immediately understood that the real question wasn't the building on the site of the Astor Hotel but the future of New York's theatrical district. That was the basic issue, all right, but it took us some time before we realized it.

People on the outside tend to assume that planning commissions understand exactly what they are doing when they make a zoning change, just as we expect that the Federal Reserve Bank, or the President's Council of Economic Advisors, fully understand the consequences of their actions. In fact, however, the issues involved are so complicated that it is hard to predict the chain of events that these kinds of decisions set off. When the Planning Commission first considered the zoning adjustments that would enable the Minskoff firm to build on the west side of Broadway, it thought more of the consequences to the City as a whole than of the effect of the building on the complex of land uses immediately around it.

Our first reaction to the building as urban designers was much more in terms of its immediate surroundings. We were concerned about the future of Times Square, which, despite its tawdry aspects, has great symbolic value as the center of night life in the big city, as is shown by the number of tourists who make a point of going there when they visit New York.

One immediate problem that we saw was the effect on Times Square of the plaza that the developer was planning in order to take advantage of the plaza bonus, which permitted a twenty per cent larger building. These plazas, encouraged by New York City's Comprehensive Zoning Revision of 1961, had proved to be a mixed blessing. They provide valuable light and air for the office towers, but at street level they tend to be dull and lifeless: not just what you want in the heart of the entertainment district. If the plaza could have been a large and splendid space, it might have generated a new life of its own, but the developer did not wish to give up his valuable rental frontage, and had planned a low building along Broadway, cutting out a triangular plaza behind that barely satisfied the zoning requirements. Some of us took to calling the building One Half Astor Plaza—a bad joke, but a fair description.

We made some suggestions about the design to the developers to improve the building's relationship to Times Square. We also suggested including a legitimate theater, to help give the area some life in the evening, after the office workers went home.

At this point the developers and their architects made a tactical error: they reacted with derision. Our suggestions were naïve, a theater was totally unfeasible; and, besides, what was this nonsense about people calling themselves urban designers and interfering in serious business?

If the developers had stuck to the argument that the City had already committed itself to a course of action, that might have been the end of our suggestions for this particular building. Administrators are reluctant to reverse even non-binding commitments of their predecessors, for fear that they will create a situation where no policy is ever considered fixed.

Neither we nor Donald Elliott were particularly anxious to look ridiculous, however. Real estate developers constitute a small community where word gets around fast; and the whole concept of urban design in New York City was too new and fragile for us to retire from the field.

The real issue was the future of the theater district

We turned to some of Richard Weinstein's theatrical friends for help, and were able to establish that our proposals about a legitimate theater were fundamentally sound. We also began to understand that the legitimate theater issue was far more important than we had thought at first. All around the theater district, developers had assembled properties that included legitimate theaters. Another substantial group of theaters was under one ownership, the Shubert interests. If the Minskoff building proved successful, all of these theaters were vulnerable to redevelopment, as all the theaters were an economic land use only because they were old and had been paid for long ago. No legitimate theater had been built in the Broadway area since the early 1930's: as far as real estate development went, these theaters were practically undeveloped land.

So what?—you may very well ask. A member of the Planning Commission pointed out that the legitimate theater had survived a transition from 14th Street during the early part of this century.

Couldn't economic forces be depended upon to rebuild the theater district somewhere else?

The answer appeared to be no: legitimate theaters today do not repay the investment required for their construction, even if the land cost were low.

In addition, the theaters in the Broadway area had become part of a series of interconnected land uses. Restaurants, hotels, film theaters and shops all benefited from each other's presence. Pull out the theaters and you damage them all. There was also a system of more subtle interconnections between the theaters and advertising, publishing and the rest of the communications industry, to say nothing of the fact that the presence of the theaters was one of the attractions that brought corporate headquarters to New York City, creating the demand for the office buildings that were threatening their existence. Broadway without its theaters would lose much of its sparkle; New York without theaters would be greatly diminished.

If theaters are so important, why hadn't the City taken steps to protect them? It could have, perhaps, as part of the Comprehensive Zoning Revision of 1961; but, even if the issue had been foreseen, the passage of that document was perilous, and another innovation might have sunk it. By 1967, real-estate interests had acquired theaters with the expectation of redeveloping them. To foreclose this opportunity would mean paying compensation, which the City could not afford to do.

It has also been shown over and over again that restrictive zoning is not able to do more than delay a really significant land use trend. Zoning can't stop this kind of change any more effectively than King Canute could keep the tide from rolling in.

Our best bet was to find a way for the developers to build new theaters as part of their office buildings, and this the Minskoff firm adamantly refused to do. They now acknowledged that the theater wasn't unfeasible, merely too expensive — but they announced that they were sick of pointless discussions with the Planning Commission. If the Commission wouldn't grant the special permit they requested, they would build a far inferior building than the zoning permitted by right. In the meantime they were taking their case to the Mayor.

An appeal to the Mayor usually marks the end of a planning commission's attempt to control influential developers. For example, when the planners in San Francisco expressed strong disapproval of a proposed large building that looked rather like an oil derrick, their mayor overruled them and the derrick is now a prominent part of the local skyline.

Mayor Lindsay, a courageous—some would say foolhardy—politician, replied that of course he would be delighted to meet with the Minskoff organization, and that they should contact Donald Elliott, the Chairman of the Planning Commission, to arrange the appointment. The form of this reply was significant: it served notice that the Mayor was not prepared to let influential developers go around the Planning Commission.

More important, at the meeting itself, the Mayor made it clear that he backed the Planning Commission's interest in legitimate theaters. He expressed appreciation for the role that developers play in the future of the city, and acknowledged the importance to the tax rolls of such a large building as One Astor Plaza. He also hoped that the developers would not feel it necessary to build an inferior design, and that the developer's prime tenants would not in fact leave New York City if the project contained a legitimate theater. The Mayor then balanced these statements by saying that he understood that it was possible to find a way to build the theater that would not cause the developer to lose money, and concluded that he hoped that the legitimate theater was something they would undertake for the greater good of the City.

After this meeting, which must have been something of a surprise, the developers authorized the architects to go back to their boards, where they prepared a very creative counter-proposal, which was presented at a show-down meeting at the developer's offices. The new building did all the things for Times Square that we had wanted: there was a lavish legitimate theater, as well as plazas, arcades, and a roof-top restaurant at a setback overlooking Broadway. There was only

20

one small problem. The office tower, discreetly vignetted in the architect's rendering, had grown to approximately twice the size permitted under the zoning.

It was a tough meeting. The developers insisted that this proposal represented their last word, and was, even with the huge increase in floor area, only barely feasible. I remember feeling very depressed as Donald Elliott and I took the elevator down from this meeting. Donald, however, was elated. "Well," he said, "I think you guys have got your theater." I expressed doubt: it was impossible for the Planning Commission to grant anything like the floor area the developer was asking for. "Oh, that," said Elliott, "that just shows they're ready to negotiate."

Donald was right and the negotiation process began. It was quite an intricate one, as the Commission had to be kept informed of each successive step. To help us evaluate the developer's claims, the City retained an architectural economics consultant, Richard Steyert, who came to each meeting armed with a pile of computer print-outs. The issues involved a number of unknown quantities. Additional office space increases the developer's rate of return; but building a larger building also increases his costs. What rent would the developer be able to get? What was the optimum size for a building, after which elevators were not as efficient? Would the theater pre-empt space that would have been rented to stores?—and so on. Then there was the question of the economics of the theater itself. How much income should we assume that the developer stood to make from it? The Minskoffs were right in saying that a theater was costly to build and the return involved high risks. If a theater books a show at the beginning of the season, and it turns out to be a flop, it may be January before the management can book a replacement. Another flop, and the theater could be dark all year, producing no income at all. On the other hand, with a hit musical playing to capacity audiences, the theater owner stands to make a substantial income, not enough to amortize the construction costs, but a significant part of the overall calculation.

In the end we arrived at a range of compensation which extended to an upper limit of a 20

The result:
a special zoning district

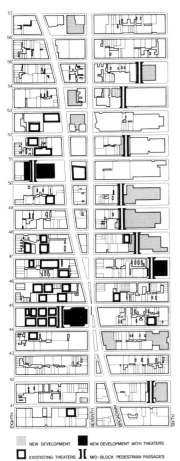

NEW DEVELOPMENT ▨ NEW DEVELOPMENT WITH THEATERS ■

EXISTISTING THEATERS ☐ MID-BLOCK PEDESTRIAN PASSAGES ∥

The theater district, showing existing theaters and the three buildings, containing four theaters, that have already been built under new incentive zoning legislation.

per cent bonus of floor area. Having decided to increase the permissible zoned density by up to 20 per cent, the next step was to find an appropriate legal means to carry out this change. For a number of reasons the Planning Commission's Counsel, Norman Marcus, felt that a special zoning district was the correct answer, principally to realize our objective of keeping theaters in a specific area.

The district would extend from 40th Street to 57th Street and from Eighth Avenue to the Avenue of the Americas. Within these boundaries, a developer could make application to the Planning Commission for an increase in the size of his building of up to twenty per cent in return for building a legitimate theater that met the Planning Commission's specifications.

You may feel that negotiation with an individual developer is a rather cavalier method for arriving at an increase in permissible density for a whole district of the City.

A most articulate exponent of this point of view was Mrs. Beverly Moss Spatt, a member of the Planning Commission, who at this time was also taking a degree in City Planning at New York University. She asserted that proper planning principles had not been followed in preparing the Theater District legislation.

It is worth stopping to consider this question of planning principles, because it goes right to the reasons why city planning has often proved ineffective in the past.

Suppose the issue of the Astor Plaza building had gone to the Mayor; but, instead of putting forward a course of action that the Mayor could back, the dialogue had gone something like this:

Mayor: Well, what do you suggest?

Ourselves: We're not prepared to make a recommendation yet. First it will be necessary to make a comprehensive survey of the theater district.

Mayor: Oh? How long will that take?

Ourselves: With luck, Mr. Mayor, about four months.

Mayor: Four months is a long time . . .

Ourselves: Then, of course, we shall need to construct and evaluate alternative policy hypotheses about the future of the theater industry. For this purpose we propose to construct a mathematical model. Now, assuming that our computer program works the first time, we shall then—

Mayor (standing up): Well, the questions you raise are certainly interesting ones. Why don't you put all of this in a memo for me, and we'll take a look at it.

Obviously, we would not have gotten very far with the Mayor if we had approached him in such a theoretically oriented manner. In order to produce an answer within the same time frame as the problem, we had to be "low church" in our approach to methodology. We talked to informed people in the theater world, and in the hotel and restaurant business, much as, you will see in chapter four, we talked to the community in East Tremont, instead of taking surveys.

We made an assumption about policy alternatives, which was that our aim was to preserve and improve upon the existing situation. Under this assumption, negotiations with an individual developer were in fact an excellent model: what was economic for one developer was likely to make sense for others as well.

While we were not in a position to assess the city-wide impact of increasing building density in the theater district, we were as conservative as possible: a 20 per cent increase in perhaps a dozen buildings spread over a period of ten to twenty years. We were able to consult with James Felt, who had been Chairman of the Planning Commission at the time of the 1961 Comprehensive Zoning Amendment, and he assured us that what we proposed was not out of keeping with the intent of the ordinance. In fact, according to James Felt, the Planning Commission had seriously considered adding a twenty per cent additional bonus for "good design" to the incentive provisions of the 1961 zoning, but put the proposal aside because there was no staff to administer it.

It was a good thing that the good design bonus was never enacted. First of all, "good design" is a hopelessly vague criterion over which parades of expert witnesses could have wrangled forever. Secondly, by not enacting another bonus, the Planning Commission left itself some bargaining power, a seam in the zoning resolution that could

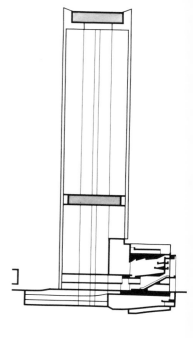

A section through the One Astor Plaza building shows the location of the theater and the way the lobby areas look out over Times Square. Photo taken from Times Square shows the glass-walled lobbies from the outside. The architects are Kahn and Jacobs; Der Scutt, project designer.

be let out in case of need, without changing the over-all pattern of the City.

The proof that we had in fact done our homework came in the political support that was generated for the special theater district at the public hearings held before the Planning Commission and the Board of Estimate. This support came not only from famous actors and actresses, important producers, and the owners of businesses in the theater district, but also from the unions: Actors Equity, and the hotel and restaurant workers.

Without this widespread support, the theater district amendment might well not have cleared the Board of Estimate, where it was opposed by the influential Shubert interests, who up to then had held something approaching a monopoly of theaters in New York.

The legislation, as passed by the Planning Commission and the Board of Estimate, was very simple, despite the complex negotiations that had preceded it. Within the special district a developer could receive an increase of up to twenty per cent additional floor area for building a legitimate theater that met the City's specifications. Each theater in the theater district must be the subject of an individual piece of legislation, known as a special permit, which must be approved, after public hearings, by both the Planning Commission and the Board of Estimate. The size of the bonus and the characteristics of the theater are a matter of negotiation between the developer and the Planning Commission, within the limits es-

A new building on Broadway, between 50th and 51st Streets, houses two theaters. One is large and of the proscenium type, the other, below, is smaller and more experimental, designed as a new home for the Circle in the Square.

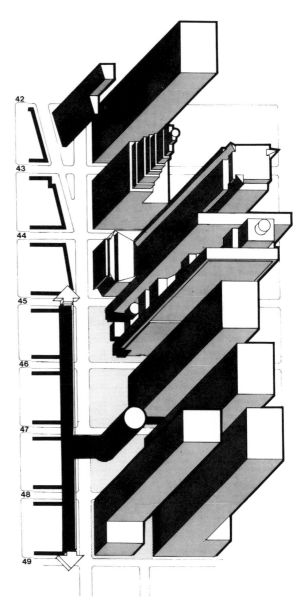

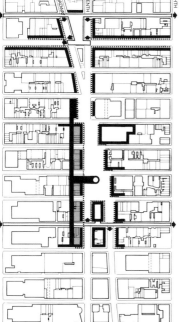

A Times Square Special
Zoning District has been
designed to give more
direction to the physical
form of the area that is
covered by the original
Theater District legislation.
This zoning district utilizes
principles described in
Chapter 2.

tablished by the twenty per cent bonus, and certain other powers of the Planning Commission to waive bulk requirements.

The Ford Foundation supplied funds for a Theater Projects Committee to advise the Planning Commission on the appropriate size and equipment for new theaters.

The theater district legislation has already produced four new legitimate theaters, amounting to a subsidy for the arts worth something like $15-million, at no expense to the public. These theaters are far more comfortable for the audience and much better equipped than any of the existing Broadway houses. Two of the new theaters are relatively small: new homes for the experimental American Place Theater, and the Circle in the Square Theater. The two others are large houses, well suited to musical comedy productions. Several more new theaters are in the planning stage, one to be located in a spectacular new hotel on Times Square, just north of One Astor Plaza.

The basic lesson of the theater district is that preservation of valuable features of the city and the creation of desirable amenities can be achieved if you can find a way to make them profitable, or at least break-even, ventures.

Another lesson was that zoning not only can provide the solution, but was a large part of the problem in the first place. The kind of segregation of land uses implicit in the concept of zoning is not as appropriate to a complex central business district as it is in the outskirts of the city. True, you don't want any chemical factories downtown, but you do want to encourage diversity and complexity.

The whole subject of zoning was a revelation to us. It had always seemed a very dreary subject, of little relevance to any creative endeavor. As a result of our experience with the Theater District, we came to realize that zoning could be made into one of the basic methods of designing cities. This discovery is the subject of the next chapter.

At right is a rendering of the spectacular new hotel for Times Square, designed and developed by Atlanta architect and real-estate developer, John Portman. Astor Plaza building can be seen in background.

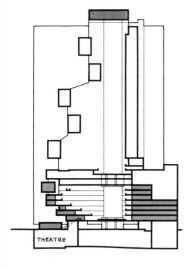

THEATRE

Section shows Times Square hotel's two huge open atrium spaces. Large size of building dwarfs the sizable legitimate theater located below grade (lower left-hand corner of section).

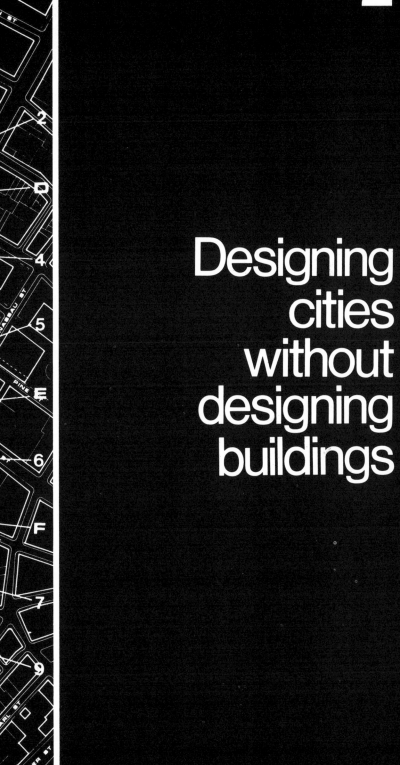

2

Designing cities without designing buildings

**How do you control
the design of cities?**

The next time you see an announcement of a new
town, or a major urban redevelopment project,
you should examine the drawing published in the
newspaper and ask yourself what will happen to
the design concept when, as is usual, portions of
the project are parcelled out to different developers and architects over a period of ten to thirty
years. The forces at work on our cities are so
diverse, and the rate of social change has accelerated so rapidly, that it is most unlikely that such a
large project, if it is constructed at all, will end up
looking much like the original design. All too
often, the merit of the published design derives
from the architecture of the proposed buildings,
rather than from any underlying coherence in the
plan itself. What if the buildings are not placed
at precisely the angle shown in the drawings?
What if materials vary; what if changes in architectural taste occur? What if changes in function
or economics force major changes in size or shape
of buildings? Will the design still make sense?

Another, more difficult question: what about
those parts of our cities and towns where large-
scale redevelopment will not occur, only a process
of piece-meal modifications on a block-by-block,
or even lot-by-lot, basis? Is there any way to plan
such areas so that they come to have the coherence
of a group of buildings designed at one time? Is
there an alternative to architectural consistency
that will still produce a unified design for a new
town or a major development?

When we went to work for New York City
we discovered that a planning process that could
achieve just such a purpose is in use every day,
but it has been the province of the lawyer, the
surveyor, and the municipal engineer; and they
have considered their primary task to be, not control over design, but over more abstract considerations of public health and welfare.

Unintentionally, however, the lawyer, the
surveyor, and the engineer have determined the
basic design framework of the American city,
through a combination of local zoning regulations
and the street pattern, neither of which has been
enacted with its design implications in mind.

Zoning is a forbiddingly technical subject
that even lawyers have a tendency to avoid if they
can, while street mapping is considered a routine

matter of little conceptual interest. As we learned more about these little-known technical specialities, however, we realized that they provide important clues to the solution of the fundamental problem of city design: how can you design a city if you can't design all the buildings?

Zoning, as its names implies, is a process of dividing a city up into zones, each of which has different legal requirements. Within each zone, regulations specify the size and shape of the building that can be placed on the land, and the uses to which buildings can be put.

The first American zoning ordinance was enacted in New York City in 1916, with the aim of imposing some minimum standards of light and air for streets, which, particularly in lower Manhattan, had become increasingly dark and canyon-like as buildings grew taller and taller. It also sought to separate activities that were viewed as incompatible, such as the factories of the garment center and the fashionable shops and homes along Fifth Avenue.

The regulations specified what activities could take place in each zone, and imposed "setbacks" on buildings above a certain height to permit sunlight to fall on the streets and sidewalks and light and air to reach the interiors of the buildings. There were also some absolute restrictions on the size of buildings in certain zones, in order to make the central areas the most intensively used districts.

City planning courses teach that zoning regulations represent the means for implementing master plans; but the first New York City zoning resolution pre-dates the establishment of the New York City Planning Commission by 22 years and the publication of the City's first comprehensive plan by 53 years. The experience of other American cities has been similar, showing that zoning first, planning afterwards is the usual sequence.

While zoning regulations are far from being a master plan, it is easy to forget, now that their use has become routine, what an enormous restriction of property rights the enactment of zoning represented. Owners of land were used to the idea that, if they owned a piece of property, they could do what they wished with it—subject at most to some deed restrictions. The legal rationale for

Zoning is a powerful design control

Studies by Hugh Ferriss show how building masses are "carved" out of zoning setback lines.

zoning is the so-called "police power" of the States to make regulations to protect public health, safety, and general welfare. The principle of the police power as a means to regulate land use was affirmed by the Supreme Court decision upholding the zoning law adopted by Euclid, Ohio, in 1922.

Prior to "Euclid," the consensus of the legal profession had been that such regulations as a uniform setback line required condemnation of the land by the municipality. This was the opinion set down in the famous 1909 plan for Chicago, based on the designs of Daniel Burnham, in which Burnham sought to apply to this most American of cities the avenues, *rond-points* and palatial architecture that Baron Haussmann had used to re-plan Paris during the Second Empire.

The portions of the Burnham plan that could be carried out directly by the City, such as the park system and the major public buildings, have very largely been realized. Where the Chicago plan failed was in the regulation of private development, because, in 1909, the only legal way to exercise such control was for the municipality to buy up the land and buildings.

For years, no one made the connection between the design objectives of plans like Chicago's, and "Euclid," with its controls based on health and safety. Architects and designers who knew all about Burnham's plan had no concept of the design implications of zoning.

But zoning, whatever its rationale and intention, is as strong a design control as any element in the Burnham plan. The setbacks created by New York's 1916 zoning changed the tall building from the straight towers of the early skyscrapers to the pyramidal masses illustrated by Hugh Ferriss in the drawings on this page. The photograph of the Fifth Avenue frontage of Central Park opposite shows how zoning determined the design of a whole avenue as surely as the vision of the autocratic Baron Haussmann shaped the boulevards of Paris.

A parallel situation exists in the case of street mapping, which also has extensive design implications that are largely unintended or based upon antiquated and stereotyped ideas. As a result, the engineer and the surveyor have had a far greater

The Fifth Avenue frontage of Central Park shows how the zoning setback lines have determined the design of the buildings.

**If a city can get
the buildings it asks for,
why can't it get
the buildings it wants?**

At top, a Manhattan block
as it is today; then as it
would look if it were fully
developed in accordance
with the zoning. Finally,
bottom, what would happen
if highest density zoning
were extended to the middle
of the block, as many
builders wish.

influence over the design and planning of our cities than the architect or the city planner. Until very recently, city governments were only expected to provide essential services, and, except among some professionals, city planning was looked upon as a form of municipal engineering, a governmental service like clean streets and city water. Planners were careful to keep their regulations within the traditional requirements of zoning, such as the preservation of light and air, or to ask for no more than was needed to supply appropriate drainage gradients and other engineering criteria. Great care was taken to appear as objective as possible, and anything that might appear in the least arbitrary or subjective was rigorously excluded from public policy.

The reason that grids of streets, all intersecting at right angles, have inexorably covered so much of our landscape is that they were viewed as rational and objective. The gridiron plan produces large numbers of lots of similar size that can readily be located on a map and meet various bureaucratic requirements for access, utility lines, and so on.

While it is easy to blame greedy real-estate developers for row after row of "ticky-tacky" look-alike houses, in many cases the combination of street grid and zoning setback lines has left the builder no alternative.

If you find the skyline of the average American city to be full of unimaginative boxy buildings, the combination of zoning rules and street grid must, again, bear at least part of the blame.

As we learned more about zoning and mapping we came to realize that, very often, the design of a new building is virtually specified by the regulations, and few new structures are unaffected by some sort of governmental control.

We are left with the question: if a city can get the buildings it asks for, why can't it get the buildings it needs and wants?

City planners and other responsible officials can no longer take refuge in a cult of objectivity and impersonality, because a decision-making process that does not consider the consequences of an action does not relieve the government of responsibility for the results. Government controls over development have become pervasive; and

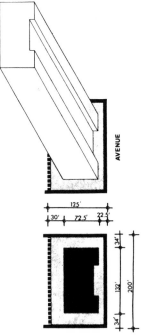

Another illustration of the way in which zoning requirements shape design. Black area is the only permissible place on the lot for the building.

they need to become positive in nature, a specification of what should be done, rather than a prohibition of what should not.

Zoning laws have been for real estate what the Marquis of Queensbury rules were to boxing. They set up rules of conduct and define what constitutes a "low blow" against the public interest: houses set too close together, office buildings that block each other's light and air, a noisy factory being introduced into a quiet residential area. Because zoning has rarely been a positive force, in the sense of shaping the built environment to a predetermined pattern, zoning regulations have tended to pull development inward, away from property boundaries, on the theory that the public interest most in need of protection is represented by the rights of adjoining property owners. Such setback and bulk controls take no account of topography, orientation, or the nature of existing buildings in the area; nor does the land use separation enforced by zoning generally take into account the possibilities created by modern construction, air conditioning and artificial illumination.

In the case of highly complex urban centers like midtown and lower Manhattan, the public interest may be much better served by the interconnection of buildings and the mixture of complementary land uses, just as, in suburban areas, the public may be better served by clusters of houses and neighborhood shopping, rather than the even distribution of single-family houses over the entire landscape.

If conventional zoning controls have so many defects, why not get rid of them altogether? After all, Houston, Texas has no zoning and it is not noticeably worse off than many another American city. And isn't zoning used as an instrument of exclusion to enforce residential segregation in suburbs? True enough, but Houston has an unusual development history that has permitted deed restrictions to perform many of the functions of zoning, and few people would argue seriously that our towns and cities would have been better off without land use regulation, whatever its defects and the ways in which it has been misused. As Richard Babcock, one of the most articulate critics of zoning, has concluded: "There is little evidence in the history of land development in America that the private decision-maker, left to his own devices, can be trusted to act in the public interest."*

*Richard F. Babcock, *The Zoning Game: Municipal Practices and Policies,* University of Wisconsin Press, 1966.

Perhaps the most important reason for keeping zoning controls, as well as mapping powers, is that they have been accepted by real estate entrepreneurs as part of the ordinary ground rules of development. The developer expects that there will be limitations on what he can do, and the cost of conforming to them is more or less discounted in the land price.

The existence of the controls thus represents a very valuable card in the hand of those seeking to improve the design and planning of towns and cities. If you can modify existing regulations to improve development, without raising the cost to the developer, you have a far better chance of success than if you seek to impose new controls that have not been part of the rules up to now. New and more stringent regulations have a way of being defeated in the legislatures that must pass them; and new rules, designed to deal with a particular problem that has suddenly been brought to the attention of the authorities, can be struck down in the courts if they cannot be shown to have general application.

We were not, of course, the only people to recognize the potential power of zoning over the design of cities. For something like a decade before we became concerned with these issues in 1967, new techniques related to zoning had been developed to control urban growth and change. The three most significant of these are Planned Unit Development, Urban Renewal Controls, and Zoning Incentives.

Three kinds of design control:

Planned Unit Development, sometimes known as cluster zoning, is used in rural and suburban areas that are being intensively developed for the first time. Ordinary zoning regulations can be suspended for a particular property, and the developer, instead, submits a master plan that, within the same over-all density, produces higher-density clusters of housing, leaving significant areas of the tract in their natural state. If the plan is approved, it becomes the development regulation for the property in question.

1. Planned Unit Development

Planned Unit Development is also at least as much a street mapping technique as it is a zoning

37

Three illustrations from the standards for Planned Unit Development, drawn for New York City by the Urban Design Group. At top, a tract of land in its natural state; center, the way the official City map and zoning requirements would shape development; and finally, the alternative possible under Planned Unit Development.

modification. In a P.U.D., only the major streets remain as ordinarily mapped, and the subsidiary access and collector streets are planned at the same time as the buildings. The result is a street layout much more closely related to both the natural landscape and the design of the buildings than the "objective" gridiron plan and the lot-by-lot development it fosters.

One of the first things that was done to improve urban design in New York was the passage in 1967 of a Planned Unit Development amendment to the zoning resolution. By that time, many other localities had been using Planned Unit Development for years, but New York's situation was unusual in that the densities permitted were two and three times the normal practice elsewhere, a reflection of the high density zoning that underlay even the undeveloped areas within the city limits.

The Urban Design Group then drew up a book of standards, to give developers an indication of the kind of site plans that the Planning Commission would be willing to approve.

Three drawings from the book are at left. A tract of land on Staten Island is shown as a contour map of its natural state, then covered by the gridiron of streets officially mapped for it, and finally as re-planned with loop streets and clustered houses that leave thirty-five per cent of the land undisturbed.

The Village Greens development, which was built on this land, follows a site plan very like the third drawing. A photograph of one of the housing clusters is shown on the opposite page.

Planned Unit Development, however, is primarily a technique for new areas where you can wipe outmoded restrictions off the books and start with a clean slate and an undisturbed landscape. Thus, Planned Unit Development is really a means of getting around zoning restrictions. For the built-up parts of the city, particularly those with high land values and successful land uses, other techniques are needed.

One such technique is urban renewal, known to its critics as "urban removal" or "the Federal bulldozer." Cities have traditionally held the right of eminent domain; that is, the right to acquire private land by compulsory purchase for

Village Greens, on Staten
Island, was actually
developed on most of the
same tract of land shown
as an illustration on the
opposite page, the first
major Planned Unit
Development in New York
City. The architect is
Norman Jaffe.

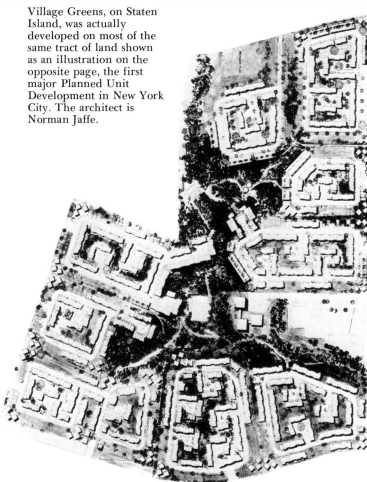

2. Urban Renewal

a public purpose. Over the years, the courts have extended the definition of public purpose to include taking land for subsidized housing; and, later, simply to create new land uses that will be more beneficial to the city. Under Title One of the Federal Housing Act of 1949, and its successors, the Federal Government has provided funds to enable cities to obtain land, in areas that meet certain criteria, by compulsory purchase; demolish the existing buildings; and then sell at a loss ("write down" the land) for developers who propose to build something that the city considers desirable.

This technique, at least in theory, offers a high degree of design control, since the municipality, as the owner of the land, can set whatever conditions of sale it likes. In practice, urban renewal plans have seldom produced good city design, for reasons we will come back to at the end of this chapter. The major criticisms of urban renewal have not been over design, however, but over the destructive effect of wholesale demolition of existing housing, stores and industries on the lives of citizens and the economic health of the city. A better understanding of the complex interpendency of cities has led to a much more humane use of urban renewal powers, which underlie the theories of neighborhood planning described in chapter 4, and the methods of improving downtown areas discussed in chapter 5.

However, there are many instances when government-sponsored urban renewal in any form does not apply. This is particularly true of areas where property values are high, and which can not be described as dilapidated, deteriorated or otherwise appropriate for urban renewal. In such areas, zoning and mapping powers remain the best potential design control.

3. Incentive Zoning

One such technique for controlling city design is the zoning incentive.

The comprehensive revision of New York City's zoning regulations made in 1961 was the first major attempt to use zoning incentives based in part on urban design considerations. Its most significant design feature was a provision that a developer could achieve an increase in floor area of up to twenty per cent, in certain high density commercial and residential districts, if he provided a plaza that met the qualifications in the ordinance. Alternatively, a smaller bonus could be given for an arcade.

Letting developers build a larger building if they provide certain desirable features or amenities is a useful principle, and it is a very valuable addition to the art of zoning regulation. It depends, of course, on the usual allowable limits being pitched to create smaller buildings than the market would otherwise permit. The bonus incentives in the New York law were introduced in partial compensation for a cut in the allowable size of buildings that in some cases amounted to as much as fifty per cent. The passage of this zoning revision was a near miracle: one of the few cases where local real estate interests have agreed to a substantial decrease in zoned density. It became law because of the leadership and persuasive powers of the late James Felt, a real estate man himself, who was then the Chairman of the New York City Planning Commission.

The new principle of a zoning bonus for plazas proved far more popular with developers than had been anticipated; but the use of the plaza bonus, by itself, has created some serious design problems of its own. While plazas have introduced valuable open space into the city, their proliferation has accentuated some of the defects of the underlying zoning, notably the tendency of the regulations to separate each new building from its surroundings. Beneath the language specifying setbacks, plazas, and open-space ratios are certain assumptions about what the resulting buildings should look like. Unfortunately, these implied architectural standards are based upon the "revolutionary" concepts of architecture expounded by Le Corbusier and others during the Nineteen-Twenties. Their vision of the city of the future as a series of towers set in parkland does not seem to be adaptable to zoning, and implementation on a lot-by-lot basis.

The 1961 zoning regulations have had the effect of belatedly imposing this concept of modernism on New York City, creating towers that stand in their individual pools of plaza space, surrounded by the party walls of earlier structures that were planned to face the street. Shopping frontages are interrupted and open spaces appear at random, unrelated to topography, sunlight, or the design of the plaza across the way.

Le Corbusier's revolutionary vision assumed that the encumbrances of the past could be swept

Le Corbusier's all-too-prophetic drawing, from the first English edition of *Towards a New Architecture,* published in 1927.

away, and cities could rise again in an entirely new form.

The process inaugurated by the 1961 zoning would take forty or more years to implement. Eventually New York would indeed become a city of towers and open space, but a city whose elements were inevitably random and accidental. No matter how well the individual buildings were designed, the city itself would have no design at all.

The elements of New York City built before 1961 do follow certain design criteria. Simple-minded as they may seem, uniform cornice lines and facades that followed the street gave the city some coherence. The old zoning rules created dreary courts and light wells, errors that the new law corrects; but the continuity that the pre-1961 zoning imposed on the street was a virtue that was not appreciated until it was lost.

Because the plaza was the major incentive provision in the 1961 ordinance, it has come to have an excessively important role in the design of the city. After all, plazas, while they make a pleasant addition to the city-scape, have limited usefulness in a northern climate, and even more limited usefulness when they are not part of a coordinated open space plan.

In the highly complex central areas of a city the plaza should be one element in a designed pattern of pedestrian and traffic movement. Other necessary elements include shopping arcades, covered pedestrian spaces (like the enclosed malls found in some suburban shopping centers), pedestrian bridges and underground concourses to allow the separation of pedestrians and traffic, and off-street loading docks to help eliminate traffic tie-ups.

The nature of the activities permitted by zoning is also important. Zoning traditionally has separated land uses into distinct zones. But downtown centers should have a desirable mix of activities, so that there are interesting places for office workers to shop and to have lunch; and some housing in the vicinity so that the area does not become dead as soon as the office workers go home. Continuous activity not only makes the city safer, but makes better use of essential services, utilities, fire and police protection, and so on. A variety of activities also creates a reinforcement phenomenon: in urban planning, or real estate, two-and-two often add up to five or six.

The 1961 zoning resolution does not provide a satisfactory set of rules for New York City's intensively used central business districts. Not only should new buildings be placed so that they do not block each other's light and air, but they should be part of a coherent, planned set of relationships that are both architectural and functional, and which are equally meaningful whether composed entirely of new buildings or a mixture of old and new.

Zoning incentives on a building-by-building basis can not supply the planned set of relationships required in the complex central districts of a city, although they can be made to be quite effective in less complicated, and less intensely developed, areas, as will be seen in chapter seven, Design Review and Environmental Quality.

A new technique was needed to be added to Planned Unit Development, urban renewal controls, and zoning incentives as a means of designing cities. The Theater District pointed the way towards applying the incentive principal on an area-wide basis comparable in scale to an urban renewal district. In New York City's subsequent special zoning districts we have evolved a new zoning mechanism, and new forms of legal controls which should represent an improvement in the administration of urban renewal as well as of zoning.

The zoning district: a new kind of design control

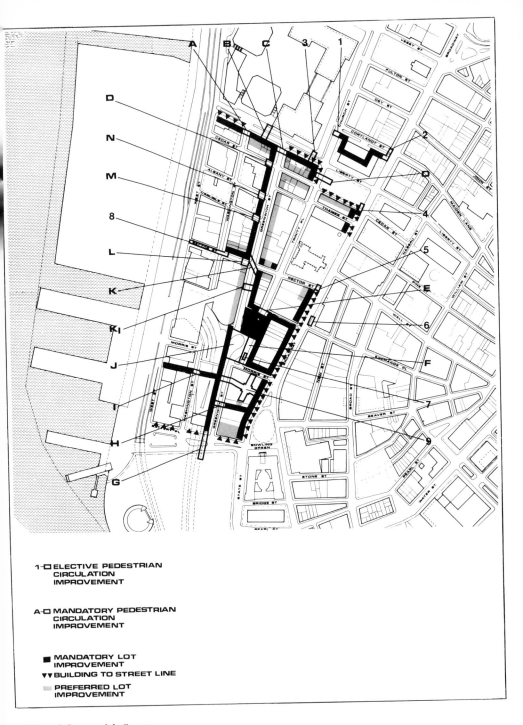

Map of Greenwich Street
Special Zoning District
shows mandatory and
elective improvements,
based on pre-determined
design plan.

The expansion of the office center in lower Manhattan confronted New York City with the need to redesign a district similar in size to a major urban renewal area like the Charles Center in downtown Baltimore, without any of the powers to clear and write down land that had been used at the Charles Center. This area has become the Greenwich Street Special Zoning District. It is bounded by the new World Trade Center towers to the north, and the Battery to the south; a landmark on the district's eastern border is Trinity Church, the church that stands at the head of Wall Street; and the Hudson River lies to the west.

It was known that considerable real-estate activity was taking place within this area, and parcels of land were being assembled; but, because of the secrecy inherent in real-estate operations, it was hard for the City to tell which areas would actually be redeveloped, what parts of the district would change first, or how far the process of change would actually go.

While it is New York City's policy to encourage the growth of its office building centers, the development permitted by the 1961 zoning within the area that was to become the Greenwich Street district had purposely been pegged at a very conservative level, so that any major change could be controlled by the City. This control would have to take the form of some kind of zoning change.

It became time for the New York City Planning Commission to make some decisions when a developer persuaded another City agency (unfortunately, City governments seldom speak with one voice) to close a small street, suddenly creating a buildable piece of land out of two plots that were otherwise too small for a modern office building.

The Greenwich Street special district was created to control this new development and it embodies an urban design plan for the whole area. But it is not like the design plans done for urban renewal areas. The designers of the Charles Center could define the exact size and shape of the new buildings, if not the details of their architectural character. Richard Weinstein, the director of the Mayor's Office of Lower Manhattan

The Greenwich Street District

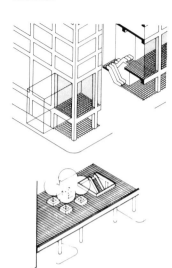

The drawings describe some of the improvements that are rewarded with bonus points in the Greenwich Street District.

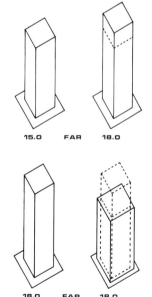

15.0 FAR 18.0

18.0 FAR 18.0
40% TOWER 55%

The developer's reward can take the form of increased tower coverage, as well as bonus floor area.

**An example of
a building in
the Greenwich Street
District**

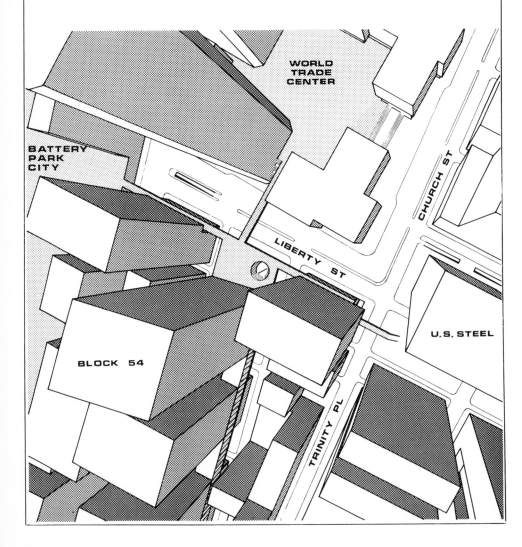

Development, had no such assurance. He had no way of knowing whether the whole district would ever be redeveloped, or which parts of it would change first and in what order. Nor could he be certain that the kinds of buildings needed, or the style of architecture, would remain constant during the development period.

In Great Britain and in many other European countries, there is a simple solution to the uncertainties created by private real estate development. The planning authorities would simply publish a general plan, and reserve judgment about individual projects until they were ready to be built. In the United States, we are reluctant to give this much discretion to our public officials, as we have not built up the same traditions of professional, and trustworthy, government service.

Instead, it is customary for our land use regulations to be published in great detail well in advance of development, so that the property owner can look up the rules and know exactly what his rights are.

Because the design of theaters involves so many complexities and variables, it would have been difficult to draft "as of right" legislation for the theater district. The special permit procedure has been criticized, however. It allows the City government considerable discretion, which makes it difficult for the public to be certain that it knows what is going on. From the developer's point of view, having to pass a separate piece of legislation for each theater is a cumbersome and uncertain process. Each special permit must be passed by both the Planning Commission and the Board of Estimate, which means two public hearings and several months in which the developer doesn't know how large his building is going to be.

Case-by-case decisions can not be entirely eliminated from the administration of zoning; but, in the United States, the aim is generally to reduce the element of discretion as much as possible.

The problem in creating the Greenwich Street district was to produce a plan that, through the medium of zoning, was as effective as the Charles Center urban renewal plan, where the authorities

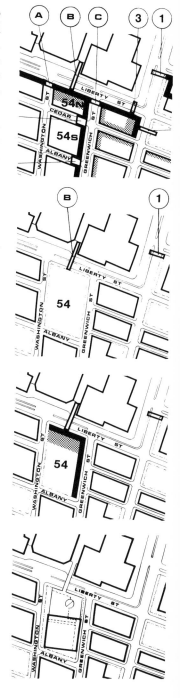

The developer of a particular parcel can look up his land in the zoning book and find out just what the requirements are.

owned the land, and could thus exercise complete control. Zoning had never been used for such a complex purpose before.

When a master plan is being drawn up as a series of buildings, sometimes the designer does not articulate his objectives even to himself, as they are all embodied in the architecture. The need to put the whole Greenwich Street plan into legal language forced the designers to define exactly what their most important objectives were.

The most important design issue turned out to be the movement of people through the district, as the size of the buildings that could be permitted is a function of the amount of congestion that the occupants and the necessary services would create.

A circulation plan was drawn showing the best possible movement pattern to create better access to the subways, and to make traffic and people move more smoothly at street level. In addition, an upper level pedestrian shopping concourse was planned, with bridges connecting the buildings to the plaza level of the World Trade Center on the north, and to the plaza level of Battery Park City, a major housing development already planned for the land-fill in the Hudson River immediately to the west of the special district.

Each block was then studied separately to determine which improvements were essential if the overall plan were to work, and which additional elements were desirable, if the developer wished to create them.

Each improvement was given a clear definition under such headings as: underground concourses, arcades, gallerias, loggias, plazas, and several different types of pedestrian bridges. These items, which all add to the developer's costs, were given a bonus value in floor area, on the same principle as the floor area bonus for plazas that had been created for the 1961 zoning revision. The increased rental from the larger building offsets the cost of the improvements. In some cases, the developer is permitted to construct a building that covers a larger percentage of the site than the forty per cent tower coverage usually permitted. Short, fat buildings are cheaper to construct than tall thin buildings, so this con-

Opposite: A building designed in conformity to the regulations shown for parcel 54 is now in construction. The rendering shows how circulation areas will look when completed.

48

49

cession is the equivalent of a bonus and is treated as such. It is possible to loosen the bulk restrictions and still follow sound planning principles because, within the district, the location of buildings and their relationships have to a large degree been planned in advance.

There are also some mandatory provisions that do not necessarily involve additional cost, which are designed to preserve the continuity of the street-scape by holding building and cornice lines.

All these provisions are designed to be self-administering, without discretionary decisions by the City Planning Commission. A property owner can look up his lot in the zoning text, and see which improvements are required and what other elements he may add, if he wishes to increase the size of his building up to the limit specified in the regulations.

The details of the text can become quite complex, particularly the language that deals with improvements connecting one building to another, as the second building may not be constructed for years.

In some cases, an owner can receive a bonus for contributions to improvements that do not connect directly to his property at all. In the event that these elements are not ready to be constructed, the developer makes a cash contribution to an escrow fund, the amount of the contribution being based on an index derived from the assessed value of sixty office buildings. The index is revised annually according to a formula that is part of the district legislation.

In addition to the incentives and controls regulating floor area, the text of the district contains rules for land uses that insure variety in the retail spaces along the concourses, preventing them from being pre-empted by high-paying but boring tenants like banks and air line ticket offices.

One of the architects designing a building in the Greenwich Street district found, to his considerable surprise, that he could not do the tower surrounded by plaza space that had become the usual formula for the "prestige" office structure. He was outraged at such interference with his artistic prerogatives, particularly when he discovered that he was up against a law, which could only be amended by the Planning Commission and the Board of Estimate. The creativity of the individual architect is subordinated to the design of the district. This principle had been debated and accepted by New York architects when the New York chapter of the American Institute of Architects supported the passage of the Lincoln Square special district.

The Lincoln Square Special Zoning District, which was the second of the incentive districts and was passed directly following the Theater district, contained the first language that specified a range of mandated or optional improvements in advance of any decision to build. Its purpose was to regulate the development of new buildings in the neighborhood of the Lincoln Center for the Performing Arts. One of the subsidiary purposes of Lincoln Center had been to stimulate private real estate development; but there was no master plan for this development, much less any means of seeing that a plan was followed.

The Lincoln Square district provides such a master plan, and was an earlier version of some of the legislative provisions embodied in the more extensive Greenwich Street district. The plan was developed through a process of community consultation, similar to those described in chapter four, and the zoning district was passed with full community support.

The design quality of this district has been somewhat diminished by a rather bizarre series of occurrences.

It was the intention of a property owner to build on a key site, just opposite the main plaza of Lincoln Center, which signalled to the Planning Commission the need to pass new legislation for the area. The developer waited until the special district had become law, and then, playing skillfully on the institutional jealousies between City agencies, induced the Board of Standards and [Zoning] Appeals to give him an additional 20 per cent floor area bonus, over the ones already permitted by the special district.

The result was that the City ended up suing itself. The Planning Commission, represented by the City's Corporation Counsel, took the Board of Standards and Appeals, represented by a private law firm, to court. The proceedings dragged on for

The Lincoln Square District

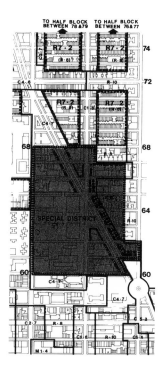

The Lincoln Square Special Zoning District was designed for the area directly surrounding the Lincoln Center for the Performing Arts.

some time, and then the City evidently failed to file certain papers by the date required. The City's case was thrown out, and the developer started construction.

The developer followed the provisions of the special district, but the building's additional bulk seriously distorts the Planning Commission's design intent. A final twist of the knife: for reasons known only to the owner and his architect, the building turned out to be covered with red and white stripes. All in all, the building was not the best advertisement for special design legislation; but the arcade and massing essential for the district concept are there, and, as other buildings in the district are built, the over-all concept will become more significant than the individual building.

The Fifth Avenue District

The Fifth Avenue Special Zoning District represents an advance, from a conceptual and technical point of view, over Lincoln Square. Like the Theater district, its basic intention was conservative. In this case it was the department stores and other retail shops along Fifth Avenue that were in need of protection.

To a visitor strolling along Fifth Avenue, the substantial limestone buildings may seem some of the most permanent things imaginable. To a real-estate developer, the view is quite different. With a map of the underlying zoning in his head, he knows that many sites along the Avenue are "soft"; that is, the zoning would permit a far larger building than is there right now. Although Fifth Avenue is Midtown's most expensive land, the demand for office space makes it economic to redevelop, which had not been anticipated when the zoning was drawn in 1961.

Again, as in the case of the Theater district, some people may wonder why the City should be concerned. Surely it is not unprofitable to build department stores, even if it may be less profitable to build them on Fifth Avenue.

The answer is that a shopping street has a delicate web of interconnecting relationships. Sever the web in one or two places, and a whole commercial district may die. This is the reason why suburban shopping centers are always planned with the small stores situated on the routes that link the major stores. Centers which break this

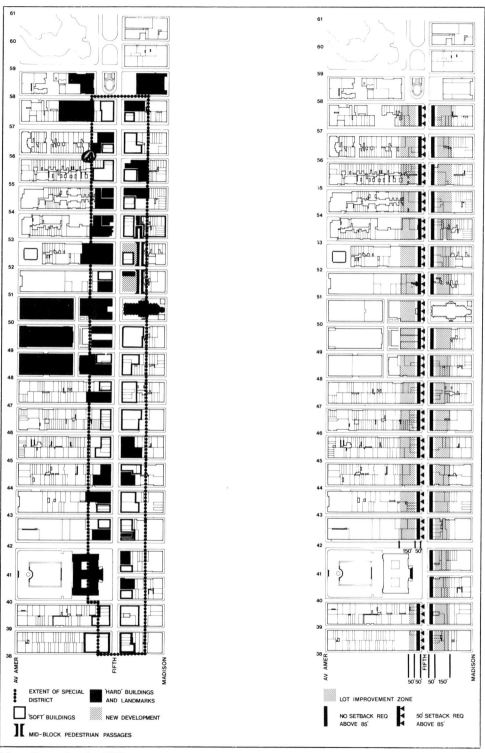

61		
60		
59		
58		

(legend, left map)

● EXTENT OF SPECIAL DISTRICT ■ 'HARD' BUILDINGS AND LANDMARKS
□ 'SOFT' BUILDINGS ▨ NEW DEVELOPMENT
Ⅱ MID-BLOCK PEDESTRIAN PASSAGES

AV AMER   FIFTH   MADISON

(legend, right map)

▨ LOT IMPROVEMENT ZONE
▮ NO SETBACK REQ ABOVE 85'   ◄ 50' SETBACK REQ ABOVE 85'

50' 50'   FIFTH   50' 150'

150' 50'

Maps show why the Fifth Avenue Special District   was needed, and some of the major provisions.

53

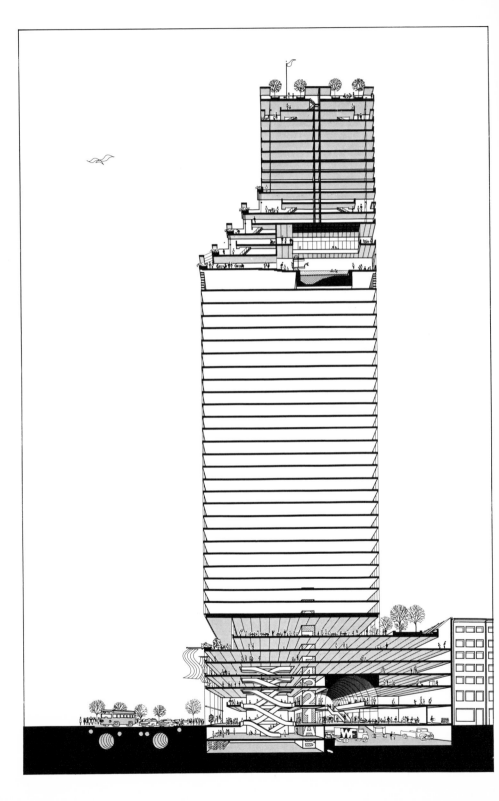

rule have usually failed; in fact, the arrangement of leases in a shopping center can mean the difference between success and failure.

On a street like Fifth Avenue the arrangement of stores has been an evolutionary process; stores that were in the wrong place have failed, or moved, and the resulting complex of shops is there because it works well in that form. If real-estate considerations not related to retailing were to dictate that a substantial portion of the street become plaza space, or banks and airline ticket offices, there would be a powerful adverse effect on the rest of the stores.

The nearly simultaneous decision of two department stores to close their doors and sell out to real estate interests alarmed both the Fifth Avenue Association and the Planning Commission. The two stores, Best & Co. and DePinna, were situated diagonally across the Avenue from each other, just north of St. Patrick's Cathedral and Rockefeller Center, in the heart of the Midtown area.

It was feared that the withdrawal of two such important sites from retail use would have very serious consequences. After several months of intensive study, Jaquelin Robertson, director of the Mayor's Office of Midtown Planning and Development, presented a Fifth Avenue Special Zoning District for review by the various midtown interest groups; and, following the appropriate public hearing process, the plan became law, adopted with overwhelming support. This was the first zoning law in the United States that encouraged a mix of residences, offices, and shops in single buildings of the downtown office district. It thus represents a major innovation in land use policy and, if it proves successful, a model for many other cities now trapped with their single-use, eight hour-a-day downtowns.

The Fifth Avenue district covers the frontage along the Avenue from 38th to 57th Streets, with regulations affecting an area two hundred feet deep on either side. The ground floor frontages are reserved for the specified retail uses, excluding air line ticket offices and banks. To strengthen window shopping continuity, the frontage cannot be broken with office entrances; and development on both sides of the Avenue must hold to the

Opposite: a section perspective drawn by the Office of Midtown Planning and Development to show character of buildings on the east side of Fifth Avenue under the special district provisions. Building is a sandwich; with lower floors devoted to retailing, middle floors to offices, and top floors for apartments and a swim club.

building line to a height of 85 feet. On the east side of the Avenue, the tower portion of the building may continue straight up from the building line—a feature designed to preserve the existing "wall" of Fifth Avenue (page 33)—while, to preserve an appropriate distance between office towers, buildings above the 85-foot line on the west side of the Avenue must be set back 50 feet. Plazas, if they occur, must be back from the Avenue, and developers are encouraged to substitute covered "galleria" space for the plaza. Office entrances and smaller, lower-rental shops would be in the galleria. The regulations are drawn so that most of them can be followed by the developer "as of right."

The bonus provisions for this district are fundamentally different from all the others. The developer can add up to 20 per cent more floor space to his building by carrying out the provisions of the district, but this extra space must be used for apartments, not offices.

This provision helps answer a criticism of special districts with zoning incentives: that the amenities and more complex land uses obtained are valuable, but that the City can't afford to keep purchasing them at the expense of increased density.

Residential and office uses are to a large extent complementary, in that they cause their peak loads on the City's service infrastructure at different times of the day. Twenty-four hour use, created by placing offices and apartments in the same district, makes that portion of the City safer and more efficient than an office building area that is deserted at night, or an in-town residential neighborhood that empties out during the day. The same police and fire stations can serve both, as can the same shops and restaurants, and the streets remain active at all hours, which is a good defense against crime.

The Fifth Avenue district not only helps preserve the integrity of a major shopping street, but it is introducing a wider variety of uses into the area; and the new shopping arcades create new kinds of frontage, encouraging a wider variety of stores. A downtown composed solely of office buildings and parking lots is not desirable either to the citizen or the real-estate developer; and, in

New York as in many other places, the very zoning regulations that were meant to safeguard the public interest were helping to change the business district into an area that lacked the variety and liveliness which is one of the city's major advantages.

It is hoped that architects will respond creatively to regulations like the Fifth Avenue district by designing buildings that combine uses and spaces in new ways, and that are not like the office and apartment sterotypes that have become all too common in our cities. The law now encourages them to do this.

Special zoning districts have taught us a valuable lesson that goes beyond zoning administration to the nature of plans themselves.

Master plans have generally been either too explicit, or not explicit enough. A typical urban renewal plan is simply a map of designated land uses, with the renewal area divided into parcels. Each parcel has its own sponsor and architect, and it is no one's job to design the whole district.

Alternatively, there can be a very explicit architectural model, with all the individual buildings carefully arranged, and every tree and path put in with loving attention to detail. Such models give the impression that all the buildings have been designed, but nothing of the sort has happened: The sponsors and architects have generally not even been selected at this point. If the renewal plan is written so that design controls follow the model, the chances are that the controls will have to be amended later, on a case-by-case basis. The result is likely to be a series of compromises that may well be worse than no plan at all.

Seeking to design all the buildings at the master planning stage is an unnecessarily cumbersome as well as ineffective technique. The planner is put in rather the same position as the legendary farmer whose house had burned down, roasting his pig, which had been caught in the conflagration. His neighbors acquired a taste for roast pig, and ever after, on village feast days, the farmer was detailed to put a pig in a house and burn it down.

Writing the special zoning district legislation has taught us a way of roasting pigs without burning down the house. It isn't necessary to

The first building to follow the provisions of the Fifth Avenue District is the Olympic Tower at 51st Street, just north of St. Patrick's Cathedral. Architects are Skidmore, Owings and Merrill.

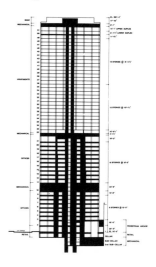

design all the buildings, if you have reached an understanding of the salient points of the over-all design, know exactly which ones are most crucial, and understand the steps required to make sure that what is most important will actually be done.

The story of the Lower Manhattan Land-fill demonstrates the most sophisticated combination of these techniques to date.

The idea of surrounding the lower Manhattan business center with a ring of residential buildings placed on land-fill inside the pier-head line goes back to suggestions drawn up by the Downtown Lower Manhattan Association and to a plan done for the City in 1965 by a team of consultants that included the firms of Conklin and Rossant, and Wallace, McHarg Associates.

The most important document that resulted from this study was an illustrative site plan (top opposite page) which showed the whole development as it would look if it were carried out in a most sensitive and architecturally consistent fashion. If all the buildings could have been constructed exactly as drawn, all would have been well; but life doesn't seem to be as simple as that.

One major complication was the decision by New York State to develop the western side of the land-fill as a separate project, to be called Battery Park City. A plan was published that had nothing to do with the drawings created for the Lower Manhattan Plan. After considerable discussion, two firms, Philip Johnson and John Burgee and Conklin and Rossant, were added to the team of architects developing the Battery Park City site plan. The result was an even more explicit and detailed drawing (see illustration opposite).

The then director of Lower Manhattan Development for the City, Richard Buford, wrote into the lease between the Battery Park City Authority and the City provisions that the site plan must be followed exactly. A capable and experienced administrator, Buford knew that, while appearing to relinquish all rights to interfere in the design of the project, he was actually retaining full control for the City. It was inevitable that the lease would have to be renegotiated.

In the meantime, the City undertook to develop the rest of the land being created along the river front. A new plan was created under the

Above: the illustrative site plan for the Lower Manhattan Plan, drawn by Wallace, McHarg Associates, Conklin and Rossant, and Alan M. Voorhes Associates. At left: the subsequent plan for Battery Park City, drawn by a team of architects that included the firms of Harrison and Abramovitz, Conklin and Rossant, and Philip Johnson and John Burgee.

■	1650
▨	1776
◩	1850
◪	1973
▦	1980

Composite map of lower Manhattan, by the Office of Lower Manhattan Development, shows how the area has been enlarged by successive land-fills.

direction of Richard Weinstein, who had succeeded Richard Buford as Director of Lower Manhattan Development. The new plan fell naturally into several parts and prospective developers were found for each one. In a complicated transaction, a group of banks with interests in lower Manhattan, and under the leadership of David Rockefeller, the Chairman of the Chase Manhattan Bank, undertook to help finance the new buildings at rates which would assure the most reasonable rents possible without government subsidy (still pretty high, however, by most people's standards) in order to strengthen the economic vitality of the whole lower Manhattan area.

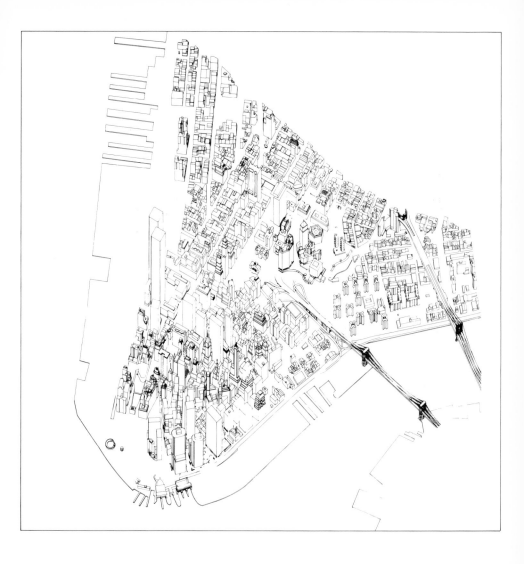

Richard Weinstein was then faced with the problem of creating design standards for all these new developments, standards which could also be written into a revised Battery Park City lease when the time came.

The basic design idea behind the illustrations for the original Lower Manhattan Plan was that portions of the waterfront which lined up with the vistas down principal streets were left clear of new buildings, preserving the traditional views of the water.

As an extension and elaboration of this idea, the special zoning district created for the lower Manhattan land-fill development defined three

Present building masses in lower Manhattan, from the same drawing sequence as the previous illustration.

basic concepts:

    Design Continuity

    Visual Corridors

    Visual Permeability

Based on these concepts, a text and illustrative drawings were devised to control the essential aspects of the new development without prescribing the design of the buildings.

Historically, lower Manhattan has always grown by land-fill, with the existing street system being extended. The result was the automatic integration of new development with old.

For the latest land-fill, it was clearly not necessary to extend all the streets, whose spacing had

Map shows location of existing buildings and design considerations governing new construction.

62

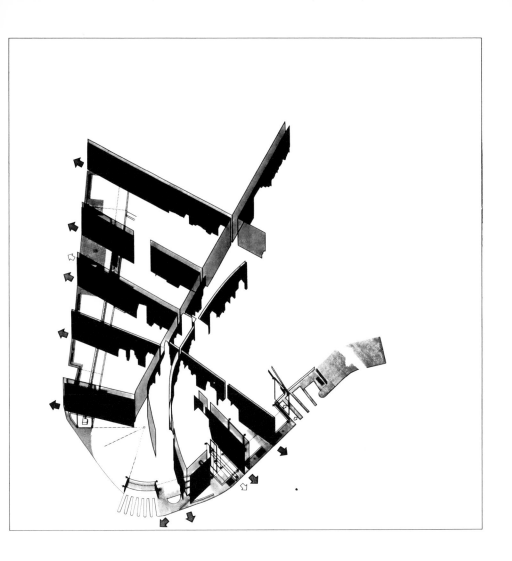

originally been set in the seventeenth century; but it would also be undesirable to have the new buildings on the land-fill totally unrelated to the patterns created in the past. The problem was further complicated by the existence of an elevated highway that loops around all of lower Manhattan at what was, at the time it was built, the water's edge. The original Lower Manhattan Plan had dealt with the highway by proposing that it be rebuilt below grade, but it is unlikely that the highway on the East River side will be rebuilt for many years; and·if it is rebuilt on the western side of the Island, it will not necessarily be rebuilt underground. Design continuity thus becomes a

Part of the design controls define planes that must be built to, and that define "visual corridors."

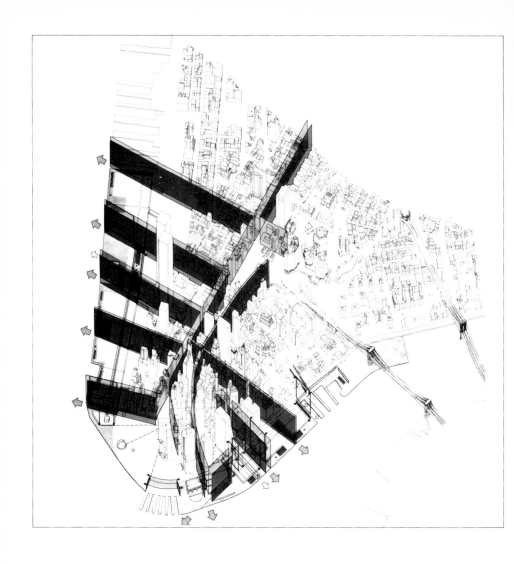

The "visual corridors" shown overlaying the masses of the existing buildings.

complicated three-dimensional problem, with the need for connections over and under the elevated structure.

The zoning district, and the new lease provisions for Battery Park City, select certain streets as significant for design continuity, and require that they be recognized in the design of new development.

In addition, the controls ask recognition of the geometry established by certain major buildings in lower Manhattan that are likely to be in existence for a long time.

The controls establish visual corridors which define areas that should be left clear of buildings,

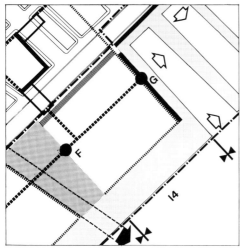

URBAN DESIGN PLAN-DISTRICT PARCEL 14

- ●▬● PEDESTRIAN CONNECTION
- ▬▬ BUILD TO LINE
- ▥▥▥ ARCADE , LOGGIA
- ⊏⊐⊐ VISUAL CORRIDOR
- ⊏⊐⊐ WINDOW
- ⊏⊐ BRIDGE

- ▦▦ ESPLANADE , PEDESTRIAN WAY
- ▨▨ PEDESTRIAN SPACE
- ▶◀ PARCEL LINE
- ▬·▬ DISTRICT BOUNDARY
- ▨▨▨ PEOPLE MOVER CORRIDOR

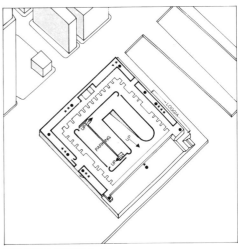

DISTRICT PARCEL 14

ELEVATION +32
- ⋆ ELEVATOR
- ● STAIR

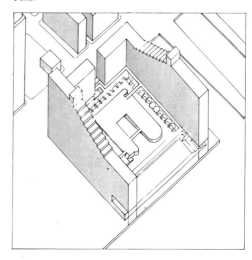

Diagram shows the way one architect responded to such urban design considerations for a particular building site. Architect is Henry Horowitz.

but also create planes that the buildings must come up to: both open space and the planes of buildings defining the space are specified.

An esplanade is also defined which will give the public the ability to walk freely along the entire waterfront.

Because the most significant experience of the new buildings will be that of people walking to them, the controls seek to regulate buildings in terms of that experience. A percentage of the esplanade, and, to a more limited extent, the visual corridors, may be penetrated by buildings if they are visually permeable, if the ground floor of the building is left open, for example.

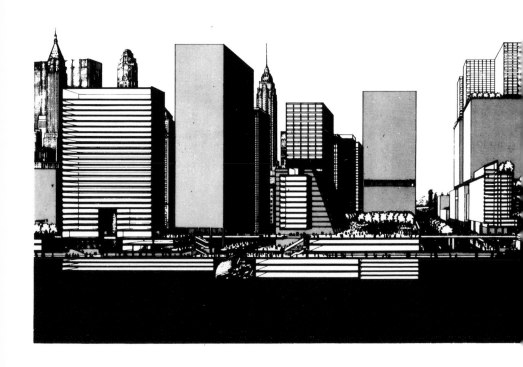

The nature of this kind of planning can be studied in more detail from the illustrations on pages 60–65.

As the illustrations show, the design policies for the land-fill relate to the design concept for the Greenwich Street district and other inland areas, so that the ensemble becomes a comprehensive plan for lower Manhattan.

The city government seeks to define only those elements of concern to the public, leaving the developer to operate as he will within these clearly stated constraints.

The elements of the plan are tied back into the pre-existing fabric of lower Manhattan, both

functionally and visually, so that the large new additions to this part of the City will help form the whole lower Manhattan district into a single unified design.

At the same time, the nature of the design controls permits the design to make sense as each increment is added; and they are sufficiently flexible to allow for modifications as time goes on.

No doubt these controls will prove to have a certain number of errors and omissions and they do not automatically produce fine architecture. They do represent a long step towards the goal of designing cities without designing buildings.

Illustrative section through lower Manhattan, looking north, shows the proposed circulation system that will connect existing buildings, at left, to future development of the land-fill, at right, a principal objective of the design controls. Tunnel is the Second Avenue Subway, which will reach lower Manhattan about 1980.

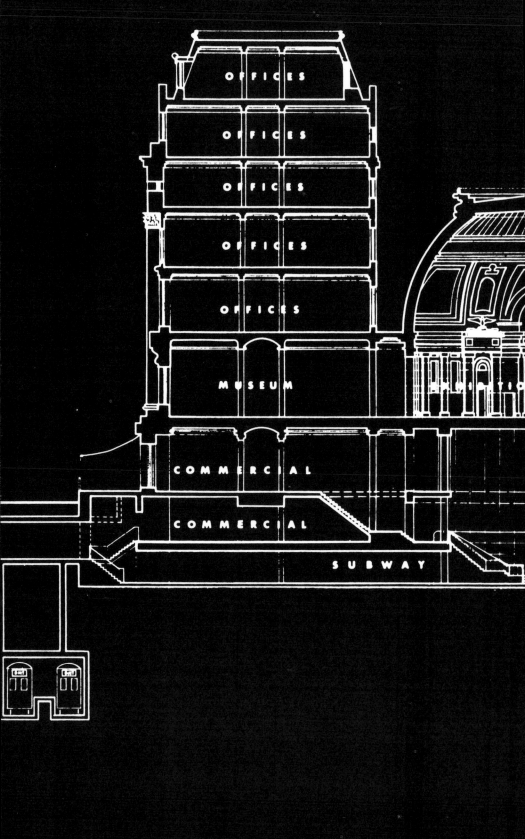

CONCOUR

3

Preserving
landmarks
and
ties to
the past

One of the drawbacks of a period of accelerated social change is that buildings planned to last for centuries can become outmoded in a few decades.

Structures of great artistic merit, designed and built with care and devotion, no longer have an economic use, and are casually knocked down and replaced. Buildings of less merit, which were nevertheless the very fabric of the city, vanish, with their accumulated memories and associations, leaving a depressing emptiness.

Both legal and architectural philosophies have contributed to the rapid erosion of the past structure of our cities.

Zoning laws, based on principles of uniform administration, make no distinctions about the nature of buildings in a zoning district. A building with a floor area ratio of 3, in a district that permits 18, is more valuable dead than alive, no matter what its architectural character.

The "Modern" movement in architecture has looked with disdain upon buildings of the nineteenth and twentieth centuries that were adorned with the trappings of earlier historical periods. Such "eclectic" buildings were outside the "mainstream" of architectural history, and so could be disregarded.

I participated, with many other architects, in the singularly futile gesture of forming a picket line in front of New York City's Pennsylvania Station in August 1962 to protest the impending demolition of this most civilized evocation of the classical past, with a train shed that even historians of "Modern" architecture thought was important. Needless to add, the demonstration did not stop the building being replaced by an office building and a sports arena.

A few months later, the architect Max Abramovitz told an audience at The Architectural League of New York that he could not understand the sentiment for saving Pennsylvania Station. When he was a young man, he added, he would have been picketing to have it torn down. When leading architects talk this way, it is hard to mobilize public opinion in favor of saving old buildings.

Transferring air rights: the story of the proposed building over Grand Central Station

The story of the proposed building using the air rights over Grand Central Station illustrates how zoning laws and unfriendly architectural philosophies make it hard to preserve landmarks.

New York's Grand Central Terminal was designed as a monument to Commodore Vanderbilt in a lavish and palatial style evocative of both ancient Rome and Napoleonic France. Its classical dress is done with great originality, however, and its functional organization as a terminal is brilliant. For decades it has been a landmark in the true sense of the word, known around the world as one of New York City's major gateways.

It was one of the first buildings to be declared a landmark when the New York City Landmarks Commission came into existence. The Landmarks Law, however, protects only the facades, and is, in any case, only a procedure for delaying demolition for two years.

Several years ago, the Penn Central Railroad decided to develop the air rights over the terminal by placing a large office tower over the existing building. The zoning permits a floor area ratio of 15, or 18 with a plaza, and the floor area of the terminal, despite its considerable bulk, is only 1.5. No plaza was possible, but an office building with an area of 13.5 times the four acre site was permitted by the zoning, a very large building indeed.

The architect, Marcel Breuer, accepted the commission to design the office tower over the terminal. An internationally known architect and a former faculty member at the Bauhaus, Breuer saw nothing incongruous in what was proposed, except that it seemed to him unnecessary to go to so much trouble to preserve the Terminal facades, which, in his eyes, were a provincial version of a decadent French classicism.

The Landmarks Commission, however, took the position that a seven-hundred-foot-high office building over the Terminal constituted an alteration to the facade, and they refused to approve the new building.

One of the legal questions raised by this decision is whether the Landmarks Commission, by its ruling, is depriving the owners of the building of the right to do anything at all with the property. If that should be the case, the City has, in effect, condemned it, and should pay the owner compensation. The City would be incapable of paying the enormous sum necessary, as landmarks preservation can not be given priority over new schools and hospitals, except, oddly enough, in Russia and the socialist countries of Eastern Europe.

Knowing that this issue would come up, the Planning Commission devised a way to give the owners of landmarks a third alternative to the choice between demolition and the status quo. It passed a law permitting the transfer of "air rights" from a landmark to nearby properties.

The result is that the owner of a neighboring piece of land can purchase some of the unused bulk permitted by the zoning on the landmark property. The over-all density of the zoning district remains the same, and the owners of the landmark can participate in some of the advantages of new development.

There are some complications, the most important being a limit on the amount of air rights that can be transferred to any one adjacent building site. The new structure that makes use of the air rights can not be increased by more than twenty per cent. This requirement is designed to prevent excessive contrasts between the landmark and an adjacent building.

This law was particularly applicable in the case of Grand Central Terminal as the Penn-Central Railroad owned a large number of adjacent properties. The whole Terminal area from 42nd Street to 50th Street on both sides of Park Avenue had originally been developed over railroad yards, to a master development plan of quite a sophisticated nature. Since the 1950's the Penn-Central had been redeveloping its properties, one building at a time, without any attempt to exploit the possibilities that such a large property holding suggests.

Using the air rights from the terminal would cause the Penn-Central to give some thought to a staged master redevelopment plan, something that they should have done years before.

The Urban Design Group prepared some alternate studies showing the difference between the Penn-Central plan and various possibilities created by the air rights transfer. These schemes were particularly persuasive at the Landmarks Commission's public hearing in pointing out the physical effect of the Breuer schemes on future development in the area: the destruction of an

One of the proposals by the architect, Marcel Breuer, for a building over Grand Central Terminal. This version would have removed much of the principal facade and obscured the rest.

72

Block model shows the area
around Grand Central
Terminal. Above, the
existing buildings; at center,
the Breuer proposal,
plus expected future
development; then, below,
the Urban Design Group
proposal, using air-rights
transfer legislation.

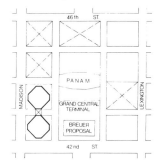

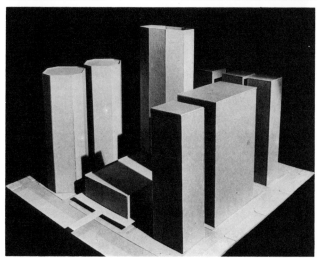

invaluable "air park" over the station itself—a major breathing space for midtown and for the Railroad's own properties which surrounded the Terminal. The Urban Design Group schemes would save the air park by transferring the development rights to a number of nearby sites also owned by the Penn-Central, so that the twenty-to-thirty year development picture would be much the same as it is today: a low and handsome landmark surrounded by a ring of new high buildings. The result would be to preserve a fine building and improve the future design of a large part of midtown Manhattan.

The Penn-Central and the developer agreed to build under the new legislation and went ahead with specific plans for an office block (also by Breuer) and a small park, both on the site of the Biltmore Hotel. This development utilized a substantial amount of the available transfer rights while "banking" the rest for future use. One reason the air rights transfer legislation was passed was that the City had come to believe that the developer would build under its provisions. However, over the next six months the office market changed; and the developer was caught in a situation where he could neither afford to build nor get out of his contract with Penn Central, which was just declaring bankruptcy. Within a year both parties had decided that it was in their own best interest to file suit against the City's new Landmarks Law as depriving them of their development rights. The litigation will probably go on for years.

There have been several encouraging examples of the use of this new air rights transfer legislation, however, which indicate that it will indeed prove a useful tool in preserving landmarks.

Preserving the South Street Seaport

The South Street Seaport Museum is a whole district in lower Manhattan that has been protected by a combination of landmark designation, air-rights transfer and urban renewal.

The Seaport Museum grew up gradually in and around the old Fulton Fish Market area. Some piers were leased from the City to display a collection of a half dozen interesting old ships, and the Museum rented space in a number of the neighboring historic brick buildings, to display a col-

View of South Street Seaport
shows the extent of the
proposed restoration. Large
building at lower left picks
up some of the air rights
transferred from the
historic blocks. Master
Planner is Jonathan Barnett;
architect, Edward L. Barnes.

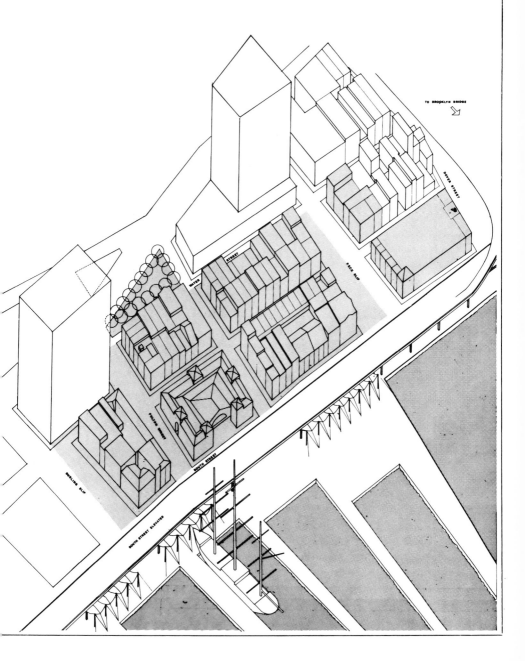

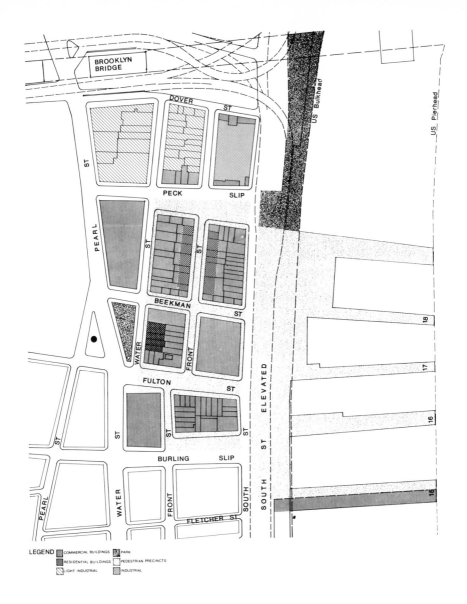

Land use plan for the South Street Seaport development.

lection of ship models, paintings and other artifacts of the sea.

It was hoped that when the Fish Market moved to new quarters in the Bronx, the buildings around Fulton Street could be restored, and a historic district created.

Unfortunately, the zoning permitted much larger-scale development; and real estate interests assembled two of the principal blocks of the proposed historic district, and made plans to tear down the old buildings and replace them with a large office structure. Imagine the developers'

surprise when the Landmarks Commission gave a historic landmark designation to what any real-estate man would see as a group of useless, run-down buildings, ripe for demolition.

Fortunately, the office building market slowed down somewhat, and there was no immediate prospect for a new building located so far from the center of the financial district. Through an interesting combination of urban renewal powers and a special air-rights transfer district, the Office of Lower Manhattan Development was able to arrange for a consortium of banks to pur-

Sketches show character sought in historic restoration of South Street area that was generally not residential but industrial. Bottom view is of waterfront esplanade.

chase the air rights over several key blocks in the district, which provided the funds to buy out the developers. This "banking" of air rights adds a new flexibility to air rights transfer.

With the major threat of assemblage and demolition out of the way, the Seaport has been able to prepare a master plan for the historic district, and begin taking title to properties and redeveloping them. The Seaport has been designated a site of the 1976 Bicentennial celebration, and is already an impressive attraction, drawing thousands of Wall Streeters during their lunch hour, and throngs of families on week ends.

These crowds, plus the proximity of a large office population and the future residents of the near-by Manhattan Landing project (see page 60), make the Seaport a very attractive location for stores and restaurants. With the air rights transferred and no longer inflating property values, it becomes an economic proposition to restore the old structures. In fact, if the buildings were used for totally commercial purposes, they might even be modestly profitable, although such commercialism would invalidate the concept of the Museum district, eliminating the attractions which draw the people who make the properties commercially valuable in the first place. What is needed is a mix of profitable commercial activities: stores, restaurants, and offices, along with museum spaces, craft shops, and studios for artists, who can't be expected to pay much rent.

The Seaport's master plan shows how such a mix can be created. The Seaport will have to raise about $5-million of the $32-million capital expenditure required. The rest can be raised through conventional mortgage loans, secured by the income of the project and other, more philanthropic loans. An area of 80,000 square feet of the approximately 570,000 involved is reserved for Museum uses, and there are sizable increments of relatively unprofitable apartments and craft shops.

These figures include the New York State Maritime Museum, which will occupy the Schermerhorn Row Block, the principal block saved from redevelopment by the air rights transfer. Because there will be a direct capital subsidy by the State, the Museum will occupy a third of the space in the block.

Opposite page: the great hall of the United States Custom House on the Battery in New York City. The Customs are moving to the World Trade Center, and new tenants must be found in order to save the building.

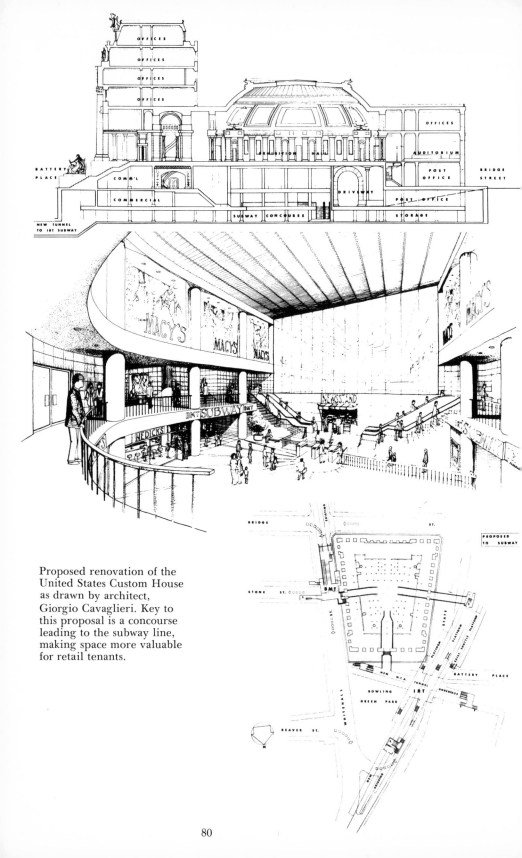

Proposed renovation of the
United States Custom House
as drawn by architect,
Giorgio Cavaglieri. Key to
this proposal is a concourse
leading to the subway line,
making space more valuable
for retail tenants.

Similar mechanisms are being used to save and restore the United States Custom House on the Battery, whose future existence is threatened because the Government is in the process of moving its Customs offices to the newly-completed World Trade Center. The Custom House is an elegant turn-of-the-century building designed in high Parisian style by Cass Gilbert; its disappearance would be a great loss.

A new life for the United States Custom House

The plan for the Custom House calls for it to be turned over to the City by the Federal Government for a nominal sum. The City, in turn, hopes to sell the air rights to the developers of a property across the street, creating the capital to renovate the Custom House for a variety of new uses, including space for a public library, the first one in the Wall Street area.

If there is no immediate sale of the air rights, it should still be possible to preserve and restore the building, using a much more commercial tenancy to carry the cost, and keeping the building active and alive. A group of distinguished members of the downtown business community have agreed to act as sponsors, working with a private organization called the New York Landmarks Conservancy, which has been created to take title to, and operate, buildings like the Custom House. The Conservancy is modeled on the more familiar conservation organizations that have been set up to preserve open space and park land.

Both the Seaport and the Custom House are threatened by the tremendous pressures for real-estate development that exist in the central areas of Manhattan, but these same commercial forces can be used to sustain and preserve them. What about areas of the City where these commercial forces don't exist?

The Atlantic Avenue Special Zoning District in downtown Brooklyn is an example of landmarks preservation in a situation where the threatening forces are much more modest, although equally dangerous, and the method of preservation can be much more direct.

The Atlantic Avenue Special District

Atlantic Avenue is lined with three and four story mid-nineteenth century buildings with fine Victorian shop fronts which have survived almost intact, because the area has been economically depressed for many years.

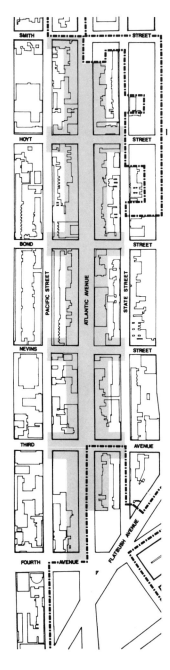

Now, however, the adjacent neighborhoods are being restored and improved as the "brownstone revival" progresses eastward from Brooklyn Heights to Boerum Hill, Cobble Hill and Carroll Gardens.

The problem is to keep the buildings along Atlantic Avenue from being modernized as they are taken over by new commercial uses, and to prevent them from being torn down for parking lots.

The interest in historic preservation on the part of the residents of the adjacent "brownstone" areas provides strong political support for the special district, which sets standards for facades and requirements that prevent demolition.

In addition to physical methods of preserving landmarks, it is often necessary to create new cultural and social institutions. The preservation of the buildings in the South Street Seaport is primarily the result of the presence of an active, concerned organization in the area. The Custom House will be saved only if useful activities can be found to inhabit it. The Wall Street Flower Show, which takes place every year on the steps of the Sub-Treasury Building, is an example of such a life-enhancing activity. Organized by the Office of Lower Manhattan Development, it has no particular purpose, except to add a bit of color to the downtown scene.

Landmark designations, air-rights transfers, special zoning districts, and private landmarks conservancies are all tools for preserving the visible traces of the past. Their application depends upon how concerned the authorities in a particular area are about historic preservation.

Fortunately, the prevailing architectural wisdom no longer considers "modernism" a more important objective than preserving a good historic building, and zoning and other legal controls can be made more sensitive to other values than the greatest real-estate return.

Most important, there are now tools like air-rights transfer and the banking of air rights that make preservation more practical from an economic point of view. However, saving a landmark is always going to be a difficult process that requires strong leadership by government, and strong political support by concerned citizens.

Above: the area covered by facade controls in the Atlantic Avenue Special District. Opposite: the Wall Street Flower Show, being held on the steps of the Sub-Treasury Building at Wall and Broad Streets.

4

Neighborhood planning and community participation

The ideal pattern for American local government is the town meeting, in which all important decisions are made in public and every citizen has a voice.

While the town meeting still exists in many localities, our big cities have grown a long way from this kind of direct democracy. Citizens seldom have any idea how and when important decisions are made, much less any knowledge of how to influence them, even if they are of immediate concern. The first intimation that many a local resident has had of an impending highway or housing project has been the arrival of the surveyors—or an eviction notice.

A system of notification in obscure journals of record and the mystifying procedures and calendars of public hearings have given a cloak of popular consent to some highly arbitrary actions, particularly when these actions have been taken by independent authorities or entrenched governmental bureaucracies which are a long way from being responsive to the voters.

The result has too often been a confrontation between angry citizens and well-established plans which have developed past the point where meaningful change is possible. If the plans go through, the citizens are left with a sense of helpless anger and alienation. If the plans are stopped, nothing may happen for years; and government becomes powerless and ineffective.

One of the things that attracted my colleagues and me to John Lindsay's first campaign for Mayor in 1965 was his interest in the decentralization of city government and in methods for giving citizens a bigger voice in the decisions that most affect them.

Little City Halls: a decentralized context for design and planning

A basic premise of the Lindsay campaign was the Little City Halls proposal. Mayor Robert F. Wagner and the 1961 New York City charter revision had created community planning boards, which are advisory groups appointed on a district basis. The defect of the planning boards was that all they could do was back-seat drive, and no unit on the administrative side of government was organized in a way that conformed to the planning district boundaries.

The essence of the proposal that we helped develop during the Lindsay campaign was to give community advisory groups an administrative unit that would be at least partially responsible to them.

All city services that were organized on a district or precinct basis would be reorganized to conform to a single set of boundaries, preferably those of the community planning boards, then in the process of being mapped by the City Planning Commission.

Each district would have its own representative of the Mayor's office who would operate as a cross-check on the delivery of city services by the line departments, and would take an active role in the preparation of long-range plans and budgets.

After Lindsay was elected, we were appointed to a task force that went into the mechanism of such a proposal in detail, preparing budgets, identifying the locations for prototype offices, and so on.*

What all of us, in our innocence, overlooked was that this proposal pulled the political constituencies out from under the City's other elected officials: the City Council and the members of the Board of Estimate, who denounced the Little City Halls as "political clubhouses" and made it clear that no funds would be forthcoming for them. Of course, what was truly worrying about the "Little City Halls" was not that they could have become political clubhouses, but that in time they might have made political clubhouses unnecessary.

The Mayor did not give this idea up, and continued to use his administrative powers to implement it wherever possible, but the immediate revision of the City's administrative structure that we had envisaged did not come about.

We were probably lucky. Proposals of this kind need to be established gradually, as all kinds of truly explosive issues are involved. For example, the decentralization of the City's school system during the second and third years of Lindsay's first administration provoked a damaging strike by the teachers' union, which saw its power destroyed if it had to deal with 32 separate school boards. While school decentralization has since been accomplished, and the head of the union now publicly acknowledges that decentralization is working, the cost has been high in disrupted

* The members of the task force were: Jonathan Barnett, Robert Blum, Felicia Clark, William Diamond, Jaquelin Robertson, Richard Weinstein, and Myles Weintraub.

schools and community struggles for power.

What had attracted us as architects and city planners to the issue of administrative decentralization was the demonstrated ineffectiveness of the old concept of the city planner who operated from outside the political process on the basis of superior professional knowledge of what was good for the public.

Enough such plans had been carried out, particularly in the area of urban renewal and highways, that the public had become deeply — and legitimately — distrustful of planners, and was learning how to organize demonstrations of opposition in order to stop their plans.

Paul Davidoff, a city planner who is also a lawyer, suggested in an article published just after John Lindsay was elected Mayor for the first time that planning should be modeled on the legal system. Every interest in the community should have its own planner and plans, and truth would emerge through an adversary process, as it is meant to do in a court of law.*

*"Advocacy and Pluralism in Planning," by Paul Davidoff in the *Journal of the American Institute of Planners*, November, 1965, p. 331 and ff.

The idea of this kind of "advocacy planning" enjoyed a considerable vogue during the late nineteen-sixties, although it never was clear who was to function as either judge or jury. In cases where the official local government is completely unresponsive to a community, advocacy planning is both necessary and an effective means of communication; but as a general method of planning for the future it seems more likely to produce controversy than results.

We were attracted to another method which calls for representatives of all the interest groups affected by a plan to be formed into a working committee. A professional then creates a rational structure for the issues and leads the working group to a consensus that becomes the plan.

This method might be called the gospel according to Archibald Rogers, a Baltimore architect who has promoted the idea of working committees and "urban design concept teams" with evangelical fervor.

Rogers had evolved his theories while developing the plan for downtown Cincinnati. As an editor of *Architectural Record*,* I had been to Cincinnati and talked to the participants, and later written about the plan.

*"A Planning Process with Built-In Political Support," by Jonathan Barnett, *Architectural Record*, May 1966.

We saw the Little City Hall and its citizen advisory boards as a perfect vehicle for creating community participation in planning over the entire city of New York. At the time, only a few years ago, such ideas were considered unorthodox by most planning professionals. Today the city planning establishment is revising its ideas to take account of "transactive planning."* It was probably easier for people trained as architects to see the need for working with community groups in reaching planning decisions, as this process is an extension of the traditional architect-client relationship.

*See *Retracking America, A Theory of Transactive Planning,* by John Friedman, Anchor Press/ Doubleday, 1973.

When the Little City Halls were not funded, our mentor, Donald Elliott, who was then Counsel to the Mayor, suggested that we find a situation where we could demonstrate the effectiveness of decentralized planning and community participation. As City funds were conspicuously unavailable, we sought the aid of a private foundation.

The J. M. Kaplan Fund, an imaginative enterprise with a long record of backing worthy causes that few others would touch, provided the necessary money, and the Institute of Urban Environment at Columbia University agreed to administer the grant. We decided to use this opportunity to undertake a prototype "vest-pocket" housing study.

The Lindsay administration had come into office anxious to create some alternatives to the traditional kind of urban renewal, which had almost always meant designating several blocks, relocating all the residents, and then clearing the site completely. One alternative, which had evolved in parallel to the Little City Halls concept, had been christened "vest-pocket housing"— a rather silly name for a basically sound idea. Instead of total clearance, the "vest-pocket" concept would use new construction selectively, placing the buildings here and there where they could strengthen an existing neighborhood. The communities themselves would be asked to participate in the selection of these housing sites.

Vest Pocket Housing, an alternative to slum clearance

Some such new approach was clearly needed. Within the boundaries of New York City there are something like 3-million individual apartments and houses. More than a quarter of them, according to the City's best estimates, are in dilapidated or deteriorated condition. No aesthetic judgments are involved in these estimates: a quarter of the City's families are living in housing that is some way does not meet the City's building code. Although the figure of 800,000 illegal housing units is staggering, similar percentages are typical of the nation's older, larger cities. For a city like Newark, New Jersey, the comparable percentage figure is closer to 40 per cent.

New York City, in an exceptional year, might build 50,000 new housing units, mostly apartments. A more usual annual figure would be 25,000 or 30,000 units, figures that include all kinds of housing from the most expensive to the fully subsidized, from large buildings to homes.

In the meantime, something like 30,000 of the City's housing units are becoming uninhabitable each year, abandoned, destroyed by fire, or cleared for new construction.

It does not take a brilliant head for figures to understand that it is not possible to renew the City's housing supply at the present rate of new construction. In many years the City is actually losing ground, its housing stock is worse at the end of the year than it was at the beginning.

Under such circumstances, it is clearly in the City's interest to try to preserve older neighborhoods, not knock them down. In addition, the city-wide shortage of sound housing has made it desperately difficult to relocate families from condemned buildings. Displaced families from one district simply increase the crowding in other areas. Families who might have moved willingly to something better, will resist frantically efforts to uproot them for new quarters which are probably as bad, or worse.

If you intend to knock down a neighborhood, it can be argued that there is little point in working with the local community, which is not likely to react favorably. Community participation in planning automatically implies a commitment to a selective renewal process.

Even so, the choices involved are painful ones; but we found that people are willing to make such decisions when they understand the reasons for them.

The district selected for our prototype study was the East Tremont neighborhood in the

Bronx, typical of many inner city areas in being in the midst of a painful transition from a modest, but satisfactory, neighborhood to a slum.

All the familiar symptoms were present: deteriorating buildings, increasing crime, over-crowding; and the population was changing from the older "ethnic" groups, Irish, Italian, and Jewish, to Black and Hispanic newcomers.

Both the old residents and the new had a strong interest in stopping the deterioration of their neighborhoods; but they were at odds with each other, and with the City, which had the usual long record of broken promises.

Also included in the planning area were two quite different districts, the Grand Concourse and University Heights. These neighborhoods had been prosperous middle income areas, but their future was in jeopardy because the old established residents had started to move out in large num-bers. The construction of a huge middle income project called Co-Op City, being built in the far reaches of the East Bronx, was also a serious threat to continued stability, because large numbers of people from University Heights and the Con-course had made applications to move to Co-Op City as soon as it was completed. At the public hearing for the East Tremont Planning proposal, the Borough President of the Bronx brought up the question of the Concourse, and the impending exodus to Co-Op City. Why was nothing being done about the Concourse? To please him, the little dotted lines on the map were extended to take in not just East Tremont, but the Concourse and University Heights as well, but no additional funds were added to the program.

When we were appointed the planning con-sultants for the "vest-pocket" housing program in East Tremont and the Concourse, Donald Elliott took us to pay a ceremonial call on Herman Badillo, at that time the Borough President of the Bronx.

An instructive anecdote by the Borough President

Mr. Badillo listened with a somewhat sceptical expression to our description of the role of the community planning. When we were finished, he decided to tell us an instructive anecdote. It appeared that in East Tremont, two nights before, a black man had inadvertently walked into a bar whose habitués had decided it was for white men only. The next morning the body of the black man was discovered beneath one of the columns of the Third Avenue El. The Borough President then politely wished us good luck, and we were ushered out of his office.

A few days later we were to see Borough President Badillo again, as he introduced us to a mass community meeting designed to acquaint the community with us and our planning project. He gave us a decidedly equivocal introduction and hastily left for another engagement. We soon found out why. The meeting was a shambles. One faction, which we later found out was from University Heights, seemed determined to prevent the meeting from happening at all. As one of their members came equipped with an electric loud-hailer, they had a pretty fair success.

Our idea of showing before and after pictures, consisting of photographs of some of the worst areas in East Tremont and the Concourse and tasteful drawings of how new buildings would look, turned out to be less than inspired. Most of those present flatly refused to believe that the "befores" were in their neighborhood at all. "Our neighborhood is not a slum" and "take your housing and go" seemed to be the general sentiments.

The meeting may have had a certain therapeutic value as a release for tension and frustration; but it did little to advance the cause of neighborhood planning.

As we learned more about the area, we began to understand why the meeting had gone the way it had. First of all, the Board of Estimate resolution lumping East Tremont in with the Concourse and University Heights may have seemed to the politicians to be a good way to get the most mileage from limited resources; but the combination did not really make very much sense. It was not so surprising that the denizens of University Heights were upset at a situation that seemed to give them the same treatment as neighborhoods several miles away, which they may never have even visited, and which they knew were in much worse condition.

Also the people who had followed the government action most closely knew that there were four other "vest pocket" housing areas, all of which were situated in the worst slums in the City. No wonder people were so concerned to say that their area was not a slum. Then there was the whole dismal record of governmental error and non-performance. How could we expect trust for anyone representing the City after the Cross Bronx Expressway and the Bronx Park South and West urban renewal projects had been planned without any community consultation, and with bad effects on the surrounding neighborhoods. Bronx Park West had been a particularly discouraging experience because the area had been designated, starting in motion a whole new process of housing deterioration, and then no government action had been taken.

When we made our first surveys we were also struck by the total inadequacy of what we had to offer: 800 new low-income apartments for an area which housed 300,000 people. East Tremont alone could absorb 10 times the allocation before you would begin to see any substantial change.

Inadequate as the low income housing was, we could find no political constituency for building even this small amount except, of course, for the more than 100,000 families on the City Housing Authority's waiting list. The older residents didn't want low income housing because they were afraid of the tenants. The newer arrivals were against low income housing because they were hoping that the neighborhood would not come to resemble the South Bronx areas they had moved away from, and they wanted to see income levels remain as high as possible. At the first meeting and subsequent discussions people were far more interested in maintaining the housing they already had than in the possibility of some new buildings which might or might not materialize in the indeterminant future.

Our original concept of neighborhood government, as part of the "Little City Halls," had foreseen an institutionalized planning function, with a council of community representatives and a full-time executive to prepare and present the issues—all the issues, not just new housing. Clearly the present situation was very far from what we had envisaged.

One thing we could do immediately was to go back to the City authorities to seek an increase of our housing allocation by several thousand units of subsized middle-income housing. This we received, with the sensible proviso that the community must accept the low-income housing in order to receive the middle-income. We also received permission, for what it was worth, to plan for rehabilitating existing buildings as well as new construction.

Bringing the community into the planning process

The next question was to find some way of involving the community in planning the housing sites. There were two appointive Community Planning Boards already in existence, one for East Tremont and one for the Concourse–University Heights area. That unfortunate initial meeting had made these Boards so cautious, however, that we found it necessary to seek a more direct community response.

We found the local clergymen most helpful in acting as intermediaries. Naturally, one believes in the separation of church and state; but priests, ministers and rabbis are often the only people around whose full-time job is to be idealistic and concerned about the welfare of their community. They responded very favorably to our concepts of community participation, put us in touch with local civic groups—where they existed—and, when there were no appropriate civic groups, set about organizing them.

We learned a lot about the composition of the neighborhoods from our meetings with community groups and conferences with community leaders. For example, we found that there was a lot more to the Italian neighborhood, called the Belmont community, than met the eye, some of which I won't repeat here. While the housing was often not as well constructed as some of the buildings that had become slums farther to the south, the structures were generally in adequate repair, and often concealed considerable affluence. The owners and tenants, in the Mediterranean tradition, spent their money inside. There was far more neighborhood cohesiveness than was manifested elsewhere in East Tremont, with even families who had moved away coming back to visit and to shop.* An outsider doing a building survey might assume that the whole Belmont neighborhood, because of its inferior structures, should ultimately be cleared for urban renewal.

*For a description of a somewhat analogous community in the North End of Boston, see Herbert J. Gans, *The Urban Villagers.* Free Press, 1962.

In fact, we found some surveys at the City Planning Commission that suggested just that. The Belmont neighborhood was actually in far sounder condition than the impressive looking Grand Concourse, whose residents were apparently prepared to move away en masse.

If you ask the right questions, a few meetings with community groups can tell you as much about the residents as a sociological survey, without insulting the residents and making them feel that the City regards them as guinea pigs, which, unfortunately, is the effect of most surveys. You can also form a good idea of what community priorities are. Garbage collection and the number of welfare families being placed in the area by the City's Human Resources Administration were much hotter issues than housing condition.

We did not find that these meetings gave us much to go on in the way of positive suggestions; it was necessary to make specific proposals. These got plenty of reaction; and, when people began to see the changes they had suggested showing up on the drawings at the next meeting, they began to believe that they actually were participating in drawing up the plans.

The Twin Parks Plan

Our final plan grouped the limited housing resources that we had to work with into two major areas, that came to be called Twin Parks West and Twin Parks East—Twin Parks being a name that had a favorable local tradition behind it. Twin Parks West was a block-wide strip along the escarpment that separates East Tremont from the Concourse neighborhood. Twin Parks East followed the frontage of Bronx Park and included the area once designated as the Bronx Park West urban renewal district.

Within these areas, sites for new housing were chosen that would minimize relocation of residents and jobs. Sound older buildings were left alone, salvageable buildings were designated for rehabilatation. Sites for new schools were incorporated into the plan, and every effort was made to preserve existing neighborhood patterns by not interrupting shopping streets, and by keeping proposals for new buildings in scale with what was there already.

These specific proposals were given a context by a comprehensive treatment plan for the whole

East Tremont-Concourse area. University Heights was left out entirely, which appeared to be the only action acceptable to that community. A special Federally-aided code enforcement district was mapped for the Concourse area. Twin Parks West filled the gap between the Concourse neighborhood, which, like most preferred residential areas, is on high ground, and Webster Avenue, a major artery down below. Between Webster and the Third Avenue "El" were districts that we mapped as areas for potential industrial renewal, and a future sorting out of the mixture of residential and industrial uses. Then we left a large gap until you come to Twin Parks East. The northern part of this gap was the Belmont community, which really needed, and wanted, little more than tree planting programs. The southern part required the same kind of treatment prescribed in Twin Parks East and West, but the necessary money was just not available. Although the Twin Parks areas covered far more territory than conventional urban renewal programs under the Federal guidelines then existing, we could not stretch the housing we had to work with to cover all the parts of East Tremont that needed help. All we could do was to recommend a second stage to the plan that would pick up these other areas.

The final plan was ratified by each of the community groups that had participated in its production, and was then approved by the official Planning Board for each district. The most difficult issue to resolve was which of the designated housing sites were to be low income, but this issue was eventually resolved by a process of trade-off and compromise.

Knowing that many people in the area did not belong to community groups, we arranged a number of store-front exhibits so that as many residents as possible could see the plan and comment on it before the official public hearing.

When the public hearings were held at City Hall, the effect of community participation was immediately evident. Instead of the acrimonious atmosphere which had greeted us at our first community meeting—and which was traditional at urban renewal hearings—speaker after speaker got up to talk in favor of the plan. No one said the

plan was perfect, and, in view of the limited resources and the variety of interests that had to be
satisfied, perfection was fairly far out of reach.
However, even those speakers who expressed
strong reservations generally added that they
understood why the plan couldn't satisfy them,
and ended by expressing their support.

A substantial amount of this plan has now
been carried out, much of it under the programs
of the New York State Urban Development
Corporation.

**Implementing the
Twin Parks Plan**

Various community organizations, under the
leadership of Father Mario Ziccarelli, then
Assistant Pastor of the Church of Our Lady of
Mt. Carmel, have banded together into the Twin
Parks Association to sponsor the non-profit housing in both renewal areas. The Urban Development Corporation and the New York City Housing Authority put the design of the buildings
into the hands of imaginative architects—including Giovanni Pasanella, who had been associated
with the production of the plan. These architects
were willing to work out the problems of designing for unconventional sites, within the constraints
imposed by housing economics and the very conventional guidelines of the various agencies
involved.

The architectural design of the new structures
in Twin Parks is much more imaginative, and
relates much more closely to the existing fabric
of the city, than in most renewal areas.

Instead of enclaves of new construction, old
and new have been re-designed into a single
fabric, and schools and other community areas
have been designed as an integral part of the new
buildings, just as specified in the plan.

The property acquisition for the Twin Parks
urban renewal areas was done entirely with City
funds, but the Federal Government, encouraged
in part by New York's experience with East Tremont and other "vest-pocket" areas, has changed
its regulations to permit Federal subsidy funds
to be used for Neighborhood Development Plans
where new construction is used selectively, and
every building in the designated areas does not
have to be torn down or brought up to the standards of a new building. In fact, N.D.P.'s, as they
are called, have become the standard procedure.

Evaluating the Twin Parks Plan

In terms of its stated purpose, building several thousand apartments, the East Tremont experience has been successful. In terms of its implied purpose, the conservation of a whole neighborhood, success is far from certain.

"Vest pocket" housing is often more costly and more complicated to build than housing on new or cleared sites. The early "vest pocket" projects, like Twin Parks, were quite a puzzle to administrators who were used to the tidy parcels created by urban renewal and clearance programs. In some cases, the effect of zoning and Federal guidelines was so restrictive that the sites had to be modified. In others, architects and administrators found ways to make regulations which had been written to cover the conventional situation work for the irregular sites created by neighborhood planning. The justification for all this additional trouble and expense is the saving in the human costs of relocation and neighborhood disruption, and in the secondary effects, particularly the encouragement to nearby property owners to make investments for repairs and improvements. Community participation did speed the urban renewal process, as did execution of the plan by the Urban Development Corporation. The Twin Parks plan was approved faster, and the buildings went ahead more quickly, than usual. From the first community meeting to the opening of the first completed building took just six years, which is very good for urban renewal.

So far, very few of the hoped-for secondary effects have been realized in East Tremont. Part of the problem has been that the rehabilitation called for in the plan has been hard to achieve, as the City does not have an effective program for aiding rehabilitation and the banks are still unwilling to make loans in the area. Unfortunately, the need for rehabilitation is becoming even more urgent, as several important buildings which were sound when the plan was drawn have deteriorated markedly since then.

A code enforcement district, the Concourse Action Program, has been initiated in the Concourse neighborhood as suggested in our plan, and it is hoped that preventive medicine will obviate the need for rehabilitation. At this writing, however, the results are not known; but such

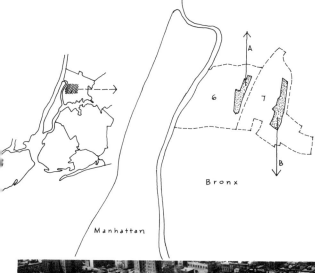

The two major areas for "vest pocket" housing in East Tremont are Twin Parks West (A, above), and Twin Parks East (B, below). The aerial photos show both areas before new housing was constructed, revealing the many places where land was vacant or under-utilized, and thus a potential vest-pocket housing site.

A sharp drop in grade along a rocky escarpment in the Twin Parks West area permitted the buildings to blend in with the prevailing low structures on the uphill side, and still be an economic size. Building above, left, was designed by architects Prentice and Chan. Below, left: the building at the southern tip of Twin Parks West, viewed from the east. The architect was Giovanni Pasanella. Building steps up in harmony with sharply sloping street on opposite side. Photo also shows prevailing scale and building mix of East Tremont neighborhood.

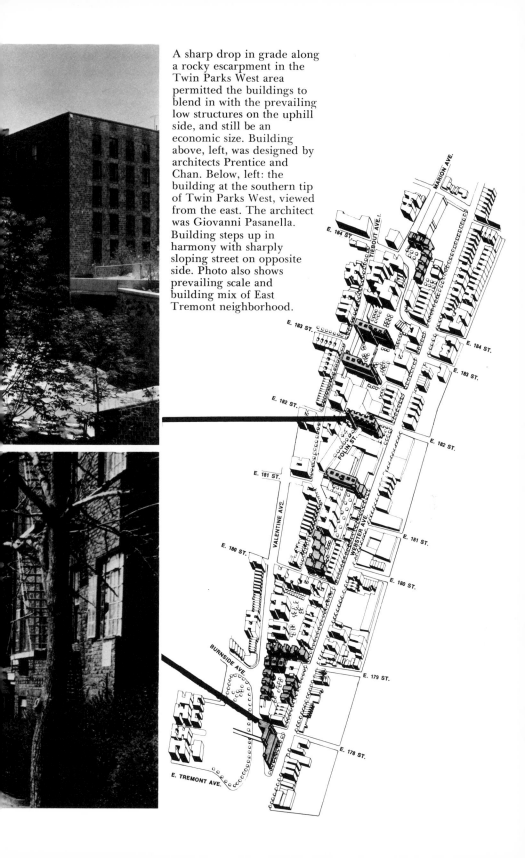

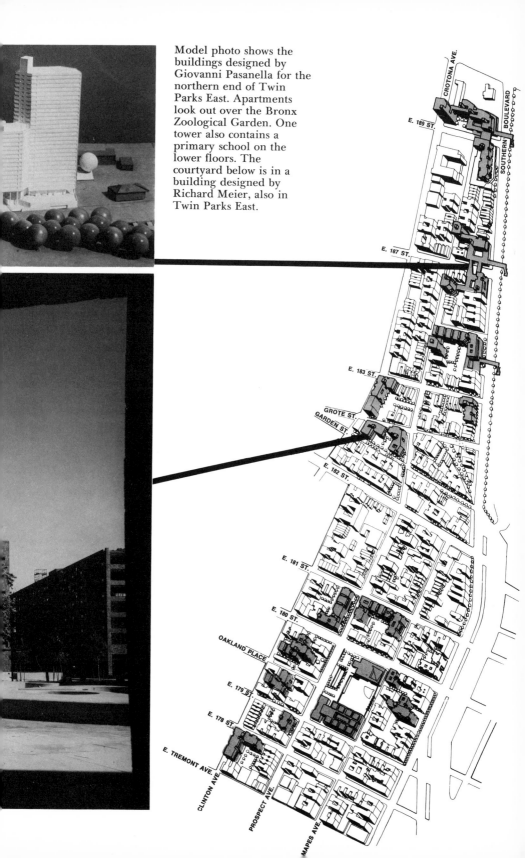

Model photo shows the buildings designed by Giovanni Pasanella for the northern end of Twin Parks East. Apartments look out over the Bronx Zoological Garden. One tower also contains a primary school on the lower floors. The courtyard below is in a building designed by Richard Meier, also in Twin Parks East.

code enforcement programs have rarely been successful in the past. Neighborhood renewal is still a new concept, and the full range of programs needed to make it work have not yet been invented.

Community participation also still has a long way to go before it is fully effective. While the community involvement in East Tremont has been real, the City and State have had a lot of trouble responding to it. The last few years have borne out our original supposition that the community will participate most effectively in the decision-making process when government is administered on a neighborhood basis. The City's Housing and Development Administration has had a project director (until 1972, George Fuller) in a field office in East Tremont, and he has struggled manfully with such problems as trying to co-ordinate new school construction with the opening of the new housing, preventing the Department of Real Estate from auctioning off City-owned land within the renewal areas, or keeping the Building Department's demolition program from knocking down empty buildings slated for rehabilitation. In each case, however, the project director is grappling with city-wide agencies that have no interest in neighborhood co-ordination. All the inertia in the system is against him.

Neighborhood government would enhance the possibility of bringing the East Tremont area back to a point where private investment could begin again. The area has many natural assets. It has a railway station that is only twenty-five minutes from Grand Central Terminal; it has slower, but cheaper, subway service, beautiful parks, Fordham University, good Italian restaurants, bakeries, and shops. The Concourse and University Heights have similar advantages, plus commodious apartments and spacious old houses. Given the right circumstances, some people who now live in the suburbs, or are about to move there or to enclaves like Co-op City, would remain in or move back to these neighborhoods, with their more convenient location and lower cost of living. All that would be necessary is the assurance of a low crime rate, good schools, and perhaps, some well-selected express bus service routes. At the moment, these sound like impossible requirements; but the underlying assets are there, all that is needed are the policies and investments to take advantage of them.

The Housing Act of 1968, along with its Neighborhood Development provisions, also includes the beginnings of a Federal policy for aiding the development of new communities. New communities created within the boundaries of existing cities are eligible for assistance under this Act. It is in comprehensive programs of this kind that hope for urban neighborhoods like East Tremont and the Concourse will be found.

The Twin Parks experience has helped us to shape some general procedures for neighborhood renewal and community participation which we have used in subsequent projects. It should be understood that community participation, in the absense of an effective decentralization of municipal administration, is always going to be makeshift; but it can be a great deal better than nothing.

Whenever possible, a single working committee should be created which includes representatives of all the relevant interest groups in the neighborhood in question. Our inability to do this for East Tremont and the Concourse cost us many extra meetings, and prevented us from going into as great detail as we would have liked with any one group.

In our subsequent experiences with neighborhood renewal after the formation of the Urban Design Group, we always made a point of creating one working committee wherever we could. In his work with the Coney Island neighborhood plan, an area with a long history of controversy, our associate, Alexander Cooper, devoted most of his efforts to the creation of his working committee, and was rewarded by finding that the planning and design decisions turned out to be relatively easy once he could get everyone in one room and willing to talk to each other.

A working committee can be elected, but these kinds of unofficial elections are generally not taken seriously by a majority of the voters. Government officials should be cautious about appointing a committee, however, as, even if all factions are represented, such committees can be regarded as a put-up job. Some of the most successful committees just form themselves, strange as

The Coney Island Plan and some generalizations about community participation

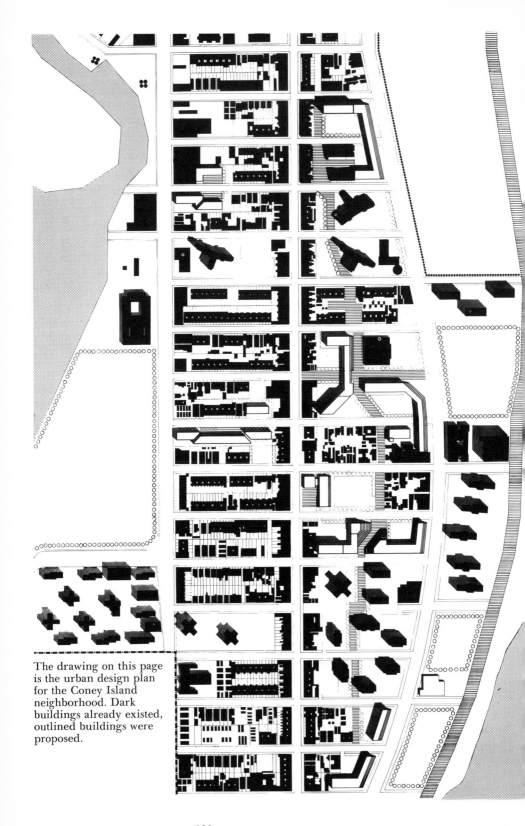

The drawing on this page
is the urban design plan
for the Coney Island
neighborhood. Dark
buildings already existed,
outlined buildings were
proposed.

this may seem. Inevitably, however, some people will be overlooked, or will not take the effort seriously. Before the conventional public hearing it is worth holding local hearings in the community to pick up the people who have been left out and to ratify the decisions of the working group. If the working committee is a good one, its members will help marshall community support for its plans.

If at all possible, the government officials concerned with implementing the plan should be represented while the committee is meeting, as it is not much use to arrive at a consensus in the community if the government is not going to follow it.

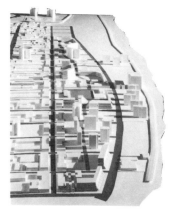

Organizing principle for Coney Island Plan was the circulation system, most of which followed a disused trolley right of way.

The planning process in the working committee should begin by reaching agreement on a description of existing conditions in the neighborhood. Sometimes a local resident, following his customary routes through the area for years, will be ignorant of conditions right around the block from his home. On the other hand, planning and design professionals, who are outsiders, may draw the wrong conclusion from their observations and need to be set straight.

Where a community committee most needs professional help is in defining the range of possibilities that are open to it. It is unreasonable to ask such a group to formulate what it wants out of thin air, with no grasp of possible alternatives. It is necessary to be very clear about the relative realism of various courses of action. If the whole planning exercise is simply devoted to showing what ought to happen in the future, without any definite appropriation of funds in sight, it is important that everyone understand that at once — and don't be surprised if interest immediately evaporates. Except in cases where the municipal authorities are hopelessly intransigent, this kind of "shopping list" planning does not serve a very useful purpose.

Community groups will accept realistic limitations, even when they don't approve of them. We agreed with the East Tremont community that housing would not solve all their problems, and that the housing allocation itself was not enough; but there seemed no point in rejecting the housing just because it was inadequate. East Tre-

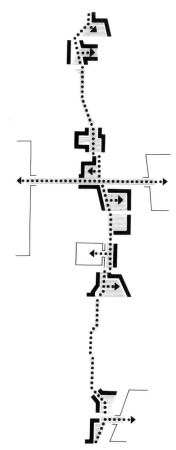

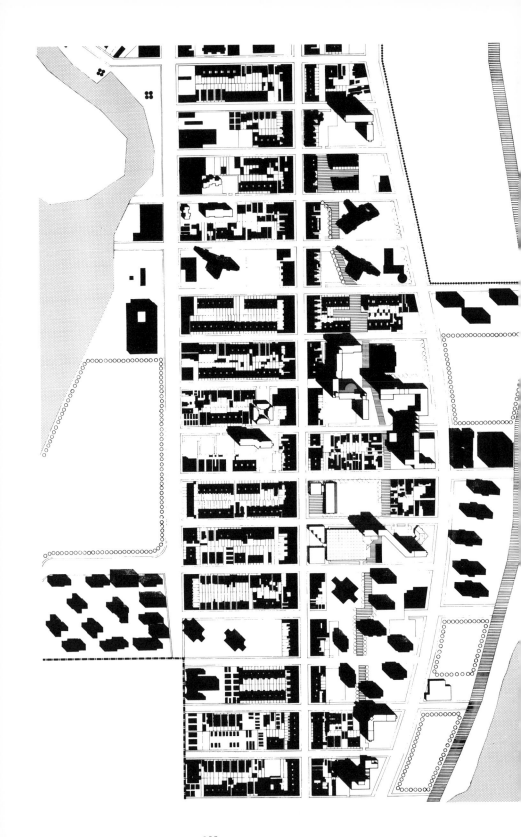

108

At left, the Coney Island Plan as built, in contrast to the concept plan shown earlier. Architects for buildings shown are Hoberman and Wasserman.

mont also accepted the proposition that the 800 units of low-income housing were the price the community had to pay in order to receive an allocation of new subsidized middle-income housing. The community's reluctance to accept income segregation by building type was not as bigoted as it may appear. A community may be far more sensitive to the subtleties of a situation that it has to live with than the well-intentioned government official. "The government" is now coming to realize that providing a rent subsidy to permit low income families to live in "middle-income" buildings is really a superior solution to a building restricted to the lowest income groups. Such subsidies are being given to about 15 per cent of the new middle-income apartments in Twin Parks, with the full support of the community sponsors.

There are always going to be some issues where the community's views can not be decisive. A locality's reaction to a proposed expressway is more likely to be "we don't need it" than "let us help you plan the best route." And don't expect a community to accept "the greatest good of the greatest number" when it goes dead against its own interest.

The Clinton Park Plan

New York City has spent years working with the Clinton community, which occupies an area west of the midtown central business district. The continued expansion of midtown commercial uses into Clinton seems both inevitable and desirable and the City is seeking ways to channel this growth along certain corridors of high-intensity use while protecting some of the existing neighborhood for lower density residential uses. In short, the City is trying to work out a long range plan some of whose features would be locally popular, others of which would not: a controlled planned development rather than piecemeal indiscriminant expansion.

The first part of the Clinton Park Housing plan is being carried out on the most expensive land ever used for subsidized housing. It will provide apartments that can be used to relocate some of the people displaced by the growth of midtown, particularly along the 48th Street corridor (see chapter six, page 160). It will also guarantee a permanent residential component to Clinton in

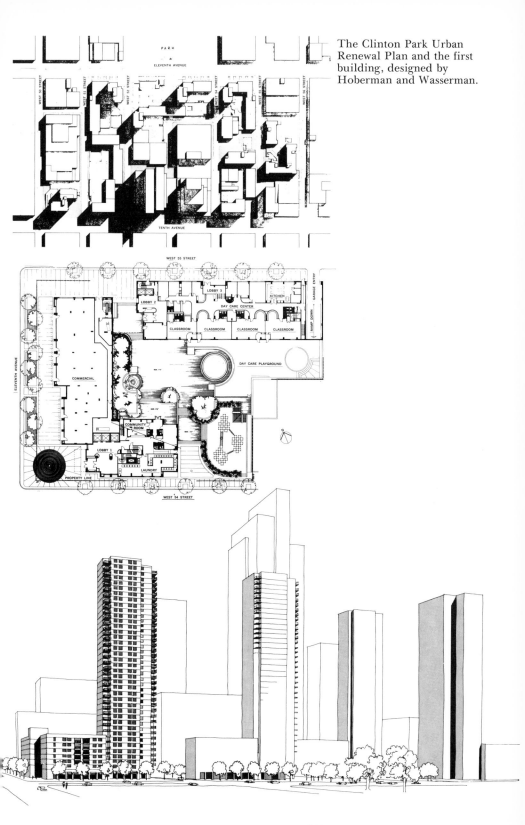

The Clinton Park Urban
Renewal Plan and the first
building, designed by
Hoberman and Wasserman.

the future. The Clinton community worked enthusiastically on the housing plans but, as other aspects of the plan developed, the community became increasingly opposed to any new commercial buildings. They wanted their new housing, which they were getting as part of a development "trade-off," but, having gotten it, they became less and less agreeable to the other conditions.

Some community participation is better than none

However, despite this kind of general anti-development bias, when a community has been consulted, there is likely to be less of the fear and hatred that used to be engendered by old-style arbitrary planning, even when the community is against what the government plans to do.

An object lesson in this regard has been the City's experience over the decision to build three low-income apartment houses on a site on the outskirts of Forest Hills in Queens. You may recall the furor that arose when construction began on these buildings. This decision, originally taken in the first days of the Lindsay administration, with the unanimous approval of the Board of Estimate, was not judged important enough to warrant the apparatus of special design studies and community consultation.

This was clearly a serious mistake, as much of the opposition appears to have been engendered as much by fear of what new project the City might announce next as by disapproval of the proposal itself.

In no case among the dozens of neighborhoods where community participation techniques have been used has there been the kind of bitterness engendered that characterized the reaction in Forest Hills. The reasons seem clear. If the politicians had known in advance the extent of the distrust the proposal was likely to create, it could have been mitigated in some way. If the community had been shown the three buildings in the context of an over-all policy that it could help create, the opposition might not have been so strong.*

The concept of neighborhood planning is continuing to take root in New York City. John Zuccotti, who succeeded Donald Elliott as Chairman of the City Planning Commission, has already shown his understanding and support for neighborhood planning and has put forward new

*For an extended discussion of community participation in planning, see Hans D. C. Spiegel, ed., *Citizen Partipation in Urban Development,* (two volumes), National Institute for Applied Behavioral Science, 1969.

proposals to decentralize further the operations of the Planning Department and strengthen the local Boards.

The New York State Urban Development Corporation, partly as a result of its experience with Twin Parks and other "vest pocket" areas, had evolved some prototype buildings for low-rise high density situations. These buildings are particularly useful for in-fill sites in existing urban neighborhoods like East Tremont. It is interesting that the U.D.C., which initially was very skeptical about small housing sites because of their apparent inefficiency, has been won over to this approach, and is building six hundred units of this new prototype in the Brownsville section of Brooklyn.

Another development that may prove favorable is the work of the State Charter Revision Commission For New York City. This Commission has reached the conclusion that the City's charter should be amended to permit a greater degree of community participation in the municipal government. The mechanism to effect this change is still under study, but may well end up being not so very different from the Little City Halls proposed back in 1965.

The chances are good that neighborhood planning will become more and more established as experience with it grows, and the understanding and technical knowledge required increases.

5

Helping downtown compete with the suburbs

We are used to thinking of the city and the suburb as separate entities, an urban center of tall buildings and a surrounding ring of leafy communities, many of whose residents depend on the city for their living. The cessation of building during the economic depression of the Thirties and during the Second World War gave the impression that this pattern of city and suburb was a lasting one, when actually it was the product of the technology of fifty years ago, and its apparent stability was an historical accident.

The widespread use of automobiles, buses and trucks has produced a new pattern: cities have spread out over the landscape and have begun to grow together, factories are leaving the old urban areas, and new shopping and office centers are growing up in formerly residential suburbs. While jobs dispersed, large numbers of rural farm workers have been moving to the old city centers in search of work, their migration the result of the mechanization of farming and, to some extent, the Federal government's policy of paying farmers not to plant crops. Welfare rolls have grown enormously and most big cities are having great difficulty in coping with the influx of unskilled workers.

The urban area has, in effect, been in the process of turning itself inside out, with people from the rural fringe moving to the center, and residents and businesses moving from the center to what used to be the suburbs.

The political boundaries of city and suburb have not changed to take account of this new distribution of population and jobs. In the early part of this century the boundaries of New York City encompassed its entire metropolitan area, including some districts that were still completely rural. Today, New York's metropolitan area covers parts of three states, and the City's population of less than 8-million is well below half of the metropolitan area population, which exceeds 20-million. On a smaller scale, this pattern is repeated in most of the nation's major urban concentrations, creating a paradoxical situation: while the metropolitan areas are growing and are economically successful, the central areas within the official city boundaries are slowing down and, tax revenues are not keeping pace with the tremendous burdens created by growing welfare rolls.

The old city centers are put in the position of having to compete with their own suburbs for continued economic health. Obviously, in a well-ordered world, city centers and the outer reaches would be under a regional government, or, at least, a regional planning authority; the economy and tax rolls would be balanced; and each part of the metropolitan region would play a complementary role to the others.

Unfortunately such a state of grace does not exist, and cities must look out for themselves. New York City, with its tri-state metropolitan area, will have a particularly long wait before it begins to participate in the benefits of regional planning.

In the absence of regional planning cities must look out for themselves

City centers do continue to have some competitive advantages. They remain the best place for offices that require a large number of clerical employees, because of their very centrality to a large labor market. The proof of downtown's continued viablity for office use is the growth of an impressive skyline in cities like Atlanta and Houston which did not have high intensity downtown areas until very recently.

Other traditional components of downtown are less obviously viable.

Large department stores have had to follow their patrons to the suburbs, or to the new suburban shopping centers. At some point the department stores have to ask themselves whether it is worth keeping their downtown stores open. If the department stores downtown decide to close, then the smaller shops will be in trouble, just as the promoter of a suburban shopping center will be in trouble if he is unable to lure at least one department store into signing a lease.

Starting with cities like Hartford, which established the precedent for using Federal urban renewal funds to make improvements downtown, cities have been taking steps to insure that downtown remains economically healthy, by encouraging new office buildings and apartments, by improving access, and by increasing the number of parking spaces. Boston, New Haven, Baltimore and Philadelphia are examples of cities with well-known, and successful, downtown renewal programs.

The growth of the office center in midtown and lower Manhattan has been so massive, because of the great size of the New York metropolitan area, that these centers have not suffered the problems of downtowns in smaller cities. On the contrary, many of the problems have been in controlling growth, and preserving valuable features of the city that would otherwise be cleared to make way for new office buildings.

The growth of these central areas, however, caused policy makers to overlook the problems of New York City's regional centers, which are small by New York standards but represent the equivalent of many major city downtowns.

The Dowtown Brooklyn Plan, improving a neglected urban center

Downtown Brooklyn in 1967 resembled the downtown of a medium-sized city like Cincinnati or Minneapolis, but downtown Brooklyn had never received the attention that had created major renewal programs in other centers, overshadowed as it is by Manhattan, and by the tradition that makes studio audiences laugh when Brooklyn is mentioned.

In 1967 there were certain clear warning signals concerning the future health of Downtown Brooklyn. While the main shopping street, Fulton Street, had never been busier, there were many vacant stores in the surrounding blocks. Also, the ethnic mix of shoppers was changing, with more residents of predominantly black Bedford Stuyvesant, and fewer whites from the outer reaches of Brooklyn, who had traditionally shopped on Fulton Street. This kind of change is not necessarily bad for business, but it does make the merchants wonder what will happen next. A major shopping center, King's Plaza, was under construction in outer Brooklyn, threatening to accentuate the process of change. A more subtle signal was the absence of a large office concentration; the major source of continued strength in other centers was missing in downtown Brooklyn.

On the positive side of the ledger from the merchant's point of view was downtown Brooklyn's status as the nation's sixth largest retail center in terms of sales, its excellent rapid transit, a concentration of four major educational institutions, and neighborhoods inhabited by middle income families that were located to the west and south.

118

Photo-montage of downtown Brooklyn shows planned new construction, Lower Manhattan skyline in background.

These middle income communities, Brooklyn Heights, Cobble Hill, Boerum Hill, Park Slope and Fort Greene, have been becoming stronger in recent years, as houses were purchased by newcomers to these areas and restored. This "brownstone revival" means that the trading area for the shops in downtown Brooklyn is potentially much more affluent than in the average older city, although the "brownstoners" had a tendency to take their buying power to Manhattan.

Dennis Durden, the Vice President for Urban Affairs of Federated Department Stores, (parent organization of Abraham and Straus, downtown Brooklyn's leading store) suggested that it was time for the Brooklyn business community to set up a development organization, hire a full time executive director, and give him an appropriate budget and staff.

Abraham and Straus and several other Brooklyn department stores, and other major Brooklyn institutions like the Dime Savings Bank and the Brooklyn Union Gas Company banded together to found the Downtown Brooklyn Development Committee, with Walter Rothschild, then the Chairman of A. & S., as its first Chairman.

I had known Dennis Durden since he was the director of a similar citizens' group in Cincinnati and I had written an article about the Cincinnati planning process. Dennis had followed the formation of the Urban Design Group with interest, and as soon as the Brooklyn organization was established, he brought their new director, Donald Moore, over to see me.

They stated that they would far rather have the Urban Design Group study downtown Brooklyn than an outside consultant, although the Brooklyn Development Committee would be willing to pay for consulting studies that we thought would be useful.

I replied that the problems of downtown Brooklyn were of the kind for which the City ought to have an answer, but that our staff was still in the process of formation, and the only person who could work on the project full time was a young architect named Richard Rosan, who planned to go back to the University of Cambridge at the end of the summer to finish his doctoral degree.

Ric Rosan proved to be a good choice. He never did manage to finish his degree, and is now the director of the City's Office of Downtown Brooklyn Development.

Our first reaction was that what downtown Brooklyn needed was a pedestrian mall on Fulton Street, and we were rather surprised when we held working meetings with the Downtown Brooklyn Development Committee and the merchants turned out to be against restricting traffic on Fulton Street in any way.

Malls are a principal attraction of suburban shopping centers, and it seems logical that providing something equivalent to them downtown would enhance downtown's competitive position.

Making the main shopping street a pedestrian mall is a concept much advocated by the architect-planner, Victor Gruen, who had drawn plans of malls for many cities. As we learned more, it became evident why malls tend to be implemented more readily in smaller cities. In a complex urban renewal situation, the mall may sometimes be the last thing you do, not the first.

As we began to understand the problem better, we realized that the land uses and the circulation pattern were badly tangled up. Property ownership was fragmentary and land values were too high for land to be assembled by private developers, given the present state of downtown Brooklyn's expectations. Urban renewal powers of the City would be needed to condemn land and unscramble the land uses, and it was important to get the deliveries to the department stores off the streets, because they were the cause of much of the congestion and confusion in the area.

The real problem was lack of design

One of our consultants, Vincent Ponte, called our attention to the potential value of the existing subway concourse and mezzanine system in creating a secondary circulation network for the whole downtown Brooklyn shopping district.

A study by James Felt and Company suggested that there would be a market for new office buildings, and the department stores reminded us of the importance of apartments, asserting that one resident family was worth ten office workers as far as they were concerned.

The plan was announced during the Mayor's re-election campaign in 1969, giving rise to justi-

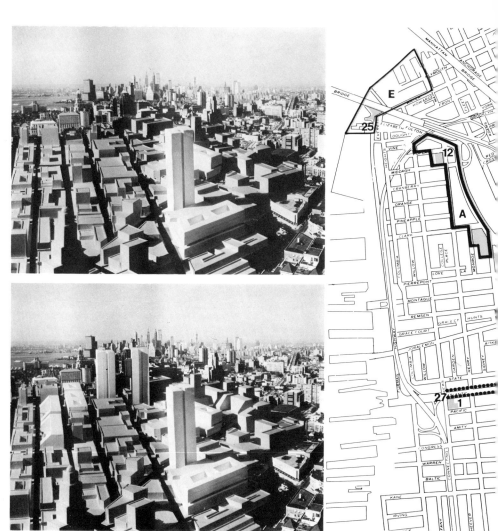

URBAN RENEWAL AREAS:
A. Cadman Plaza
B. Schermerhorn-Pacific
C. Brooklyn Center
D. Atlantic Terminal

TENTATIVE PROJECT AREAS:
E. Fulton Ferry
F. Myrtle Avenue
G. Albee Square
H. Hoyt-Schermerhorn Retail

Downtown Brooklyn plan
was presented to the public
in 1969 as a three-stage
development: 1975, 1980,
1985. Plan is ahead of
schedule.

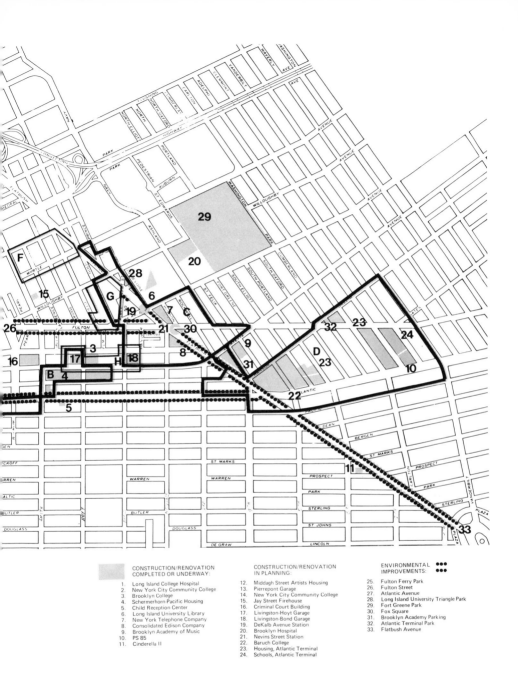

Implementation of the
Downtown Brooklyn plan
required the governmental
actions shown on this map.

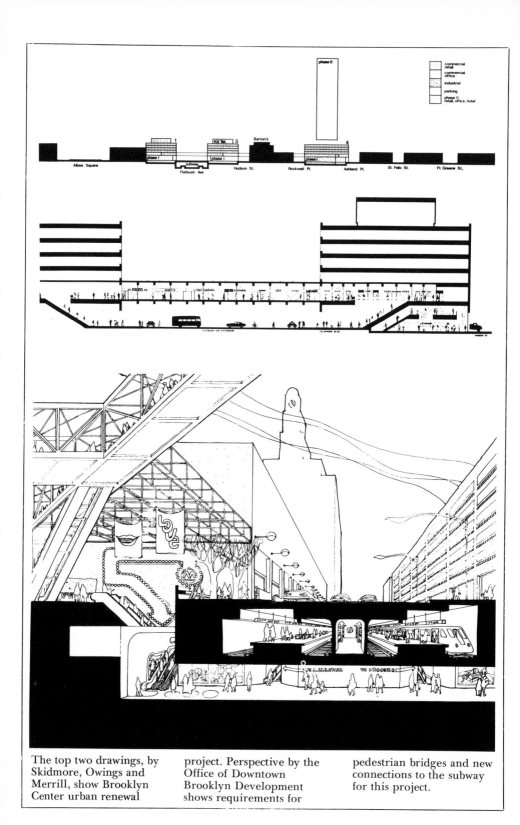

The top two drawings, by Skidmore, Owings and Merrill, show Brooklyn Center urban renewal project. Perspective by the Office of Downtown Brooklyn Development shows requirements for pedestrian bridges and new connections to the subway for this project.

fiable suspicions that it was just an election-year gimmick and nothing much would be heard of it again. The fact is that the plan is being implemented very much as it was described and is actually running ahead of schedule.

The 1969 presentation showed three stages. In the first, labeled 1975, two new office buildings would be built at the east end of Fulton Street, after land had been put together through urban renewal. It was pointed out that there would be no "write-down"; what was needed was the City's power of assemblage, not a development subsidy. There would also be off-street truck docks in a new City parking garage to be built just off Fulton Street, and another off-street loading facility just behind Abraham and Straus. All of these elements of the plan have been implemented.

The implementation process proved to be far more difficult than the planning process, however, and we spent the best part of a year casting about for ways to make the plan a reality.

Finding a way to implement the plan

New York City had no pre-existing agency whose job was to do commercial urban renewal. The City's Housing and Development Administration was primarily an agency to build housing, while the City's Economic Development Administration had concentrated on industrial problems, either plant expansion or new industrial parks. This situation was the natural result of the fact that midtown and lower Manhattan did not need government-sponsored renewal programs, and the City had never made commercial renewal plans for its regional centers up to this time.

Because no agency had complete jurisdiction, there was quite a lot of inter-agency squabbling, and deciding who was to do what required the exercise of considerable tact. Ultimately, Donald Elliott devised a solution in which a special Office of Downtown Brooklyn Development was created, in the Mayor's Office, with staff seconded from the City's two development agencies and from the City Planning Department. The first director of the office was from the Economic Development Administration, reflecting the fact that E.D.A. was managing the city-sponsored urban renewal project at the eastern end of Fulton Street. Richard Rosan went over to this office as head of planning and design, and ultimately became the director.

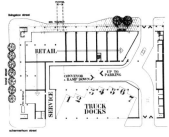

City-sponsored parking garage has loading docks for department stores one block away on Fulton Street, connection is made by tunnel. Stores in garage hold important retail frontage, allow stores formerly on the site to come back.

Having a special office whose basic responsibility was solely for downtown Brooklyn proved to be a better solution than handing the plan over to a single City agency. The reason was that the plan required the co-ordination of many agencies. For example, the concept of placing truck docks in a city-sponsored parking garage, providing off-street service to several stores on Fulton Street, was easy enough to draw on a map but very complex in reality. The garage was a project of the Department of Traffic, with the plans being drawn under the supervision of the Department of Public Works. Alterations in the plans required the agreement of the City's Budget Bureau, and then the approval of a Capital Budget amendment by the Planning Commission and the Board of Estimate. In the end, to simplify things slightly, the garage was done as a "turn-key" project for a lump sum by a private developer. Then there were all the legal questions involved in connecting the garage to the stores, agreeing on appropriate charges and so forth. As the garage was not part of the renewal area, only a special office could have seen the garage through to a satisfactory resolution. It took at least one man-day a week for the best part of two years.

The Office of Downtown Brooklyn Development also has to do much urban design work, esentially to determine the shape and form of the connections between individual projects.

The office buildings in the urban renewal district have been designed by Skidmore Owings & Merrill, but the design of certain connections to the subway, the dimensions of arcades, the character of pedestrian bridges has all been determined in advance by urban designers in the downtown Brooklyn office, and incorporated in a special zoning district similar in many respects to the Greenwich Street Special Zoning District (see page 45). Many of these matters were also covered in the urban renewal controls embodied in a long-term lease, but the zoning district covers a larger area, and also provides insurance if the development should change hands before completion.

Several other parts of the Downtown Brooklyn Plan, which had not been scheduled until 1980, have also been implemented, including 1750

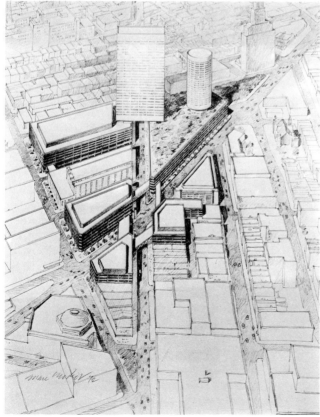

The photo shows the first completed office building in the Brooklyn Center project; architects are Skidmore, Owings and Merrill, who also made the sketch of future Brooklyn Center Development. Intersection of Fulton and Flatbush Avenues is ringed by pedestrian bridges, as shown on page 124. This development serves as a terminus for one end of the shopping section of Fulton Street, with Borough Hall and the Brooklyn government center at the other.

units of middle, moderate and low income housing on a five-block site on Schermerhorn Street, south of the main shopping area. This housing, designed by Benjamin Thompson & Associates, adjoins a major subway mezzanine at the Hoyt-Schermerhorn Station. The City's Office of Downtown Brooklyn Development has prepared a plan for connecting this housing through the mezzanine to the basement level of the Fulton Street stores, and ultimately to the concourse systems of other subway stations in the area. This plan represents a considerable development and refinement of the concept first presented in 1969. It received a First Design Award from Progressive Architecture Magazine in 1973.

Again, the design of the buildings is by a private architect, with the urban design plan giving only the most general and preliminary guidelines. However, the connections between

A large strip of vacant land right behind the Fulton Street shopping center had been created by the construction of a subway mezzanine in the 1930's. New housing on this land will take advantage of its good location and will reinforce the shopping center.

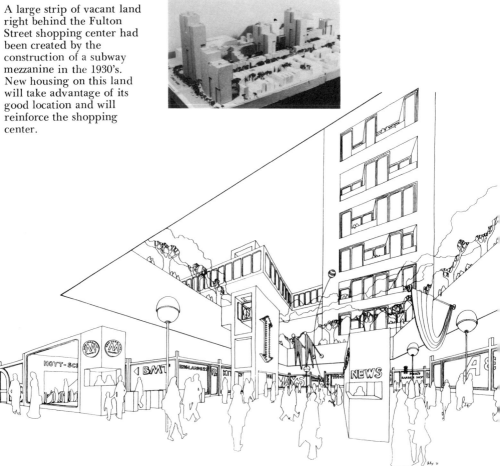

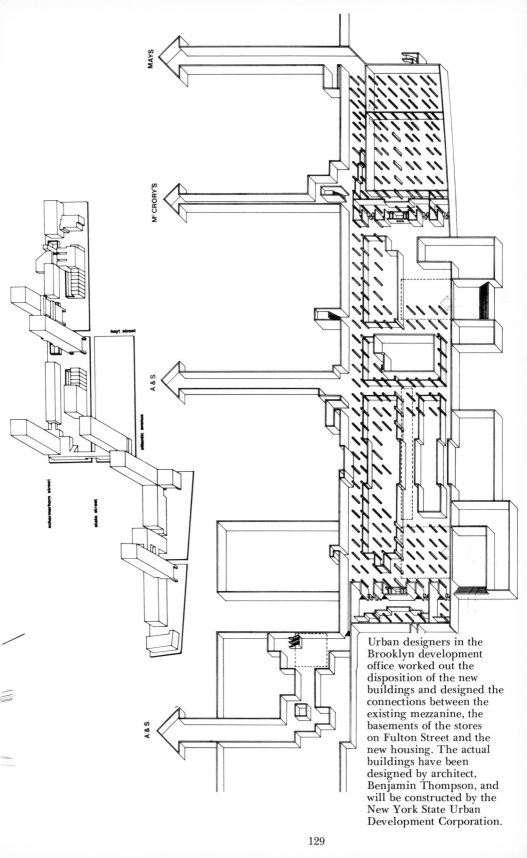

Urban designers in the
Brooklyn development
office worked out the
disposition of the new
buildings and designed the
connections between the
existing mezzanine, the
basements of the stores
on Fulton Street and the
new housing. The actual
buildings have been
designed by architect,
Benjamin Thompson, and
will be constructed by the
New York State Urban
Development Corporation.

these buildings and the rest of downtown Brooklyn are the primary responsibility of the City's urban designers, who have studied them in great detail.

Now that the Downtown Brooklyn plan is so far advanced, with new buildings constructed and tangible circulation improvements under way, the merchants are ready to consider the benefits of a Fulton Street Mall, with Fulton Street reserved for pedestrians and buses. The mall thus becomes part of the culmination of the redesign of Downtown Brooklyn, rather than the first step.

Rendering of proposed Fulton Street transitway shows widened sidewalks and traffic restricted to buses.

An analogous approach to redevelopment planning has been taking place in other New York City regional centers, notably Jamaica Center, in Queens, and Fordham Road in the Bronx. Plans are being advanced for similar efforts in St. George, the principal center of Staten Island, and Main Street, Flushing, another major downtown in Queens.

Photo-montage shows proposed redevelopment of downtown Jamaica. Existing retail center is at left, proposed office complex in center, and the York College campus at right. Perspective by the Regional Plan Association shows slightly different version of office complex. Long distances between the parts of this center will make the plan hard to implement, as mutual reinforcement is diminished.

131

The tremendous surge of office building construction in midtown Manhattan makes this area's problems different from most other centers, but it still requires a comprehensive planning approach, not unlike that used in downtown Brooklyn, but adapted to the far greater complexities of the largest central business district in the country.

Some of the individual aspects of the strategic plans developed for midtown have been described in other chapters; the Fifth Avenue Special Zoning District to help conserve the main shopping street is described in chapter two, the special Theater District in chapter one, the west midtown development and convention center plan in chapter six.

A major problem common to all these areas, indeed to central business districts in every city, is increasing traffic congestion. In 1969 Mayor Lindsay asked the Office of Midtown Planning Development to undertake a study that would sort out the traffic patterns in midtown and show how to reduce congestion to more manageable proportions. Van Ginkel Associates of Montreal were retained as the prime consultants, and, after over a year of intensive work, published an exhaustive study entitled "Movement in Midtown."

The most significant conclusions were that the entire circulation system in midtown, for people, vehicles, and goods, needed to be redesigned to reflect the actual density of development and the kind of trips being made. Arterial traffic should be separated from local traffic and channeled along specific peripheral and crosstown corridors, while private automobiles and taxis should be kept out of the areas where the number of pedestrians is greatest. Additional pedestrian space would be created in these "restricted traffic zones" by widening the sidewalks

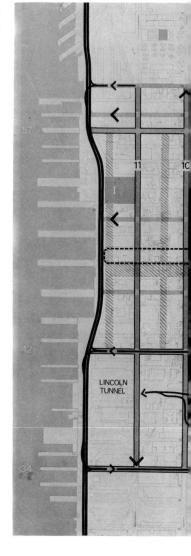

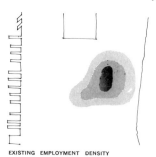

EXISTING EMPLOYMENT DENSITY

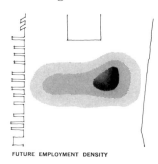

FUTURE EMPLOYMENT DENSITY

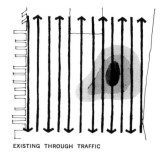

EXISTING THROUGH TRAFFIC

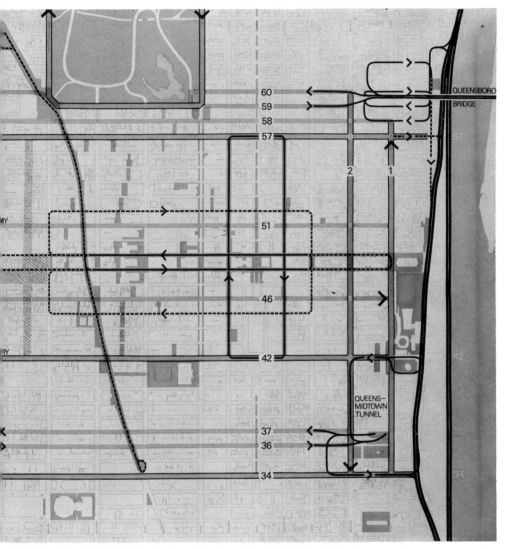

Map and diagrams explain comprehensive traffic plan for midtown Manhattan, designed for New York City by Van Ginkel Associates.

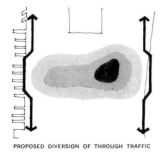

PROPOSED DIVERSION OF THROUGH TRAFFIC

EXISTING ENTRIES AND EXITS

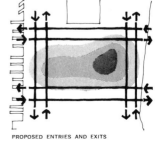

PROPOSED ENTRIES AND EXITS

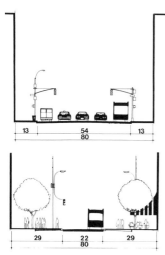

Transit way or mall proposed for Madison Avenue, with the sidewalks widened, and traffic restricted to one lane of buses in either direction, plus deliveries at certain restricted hours.

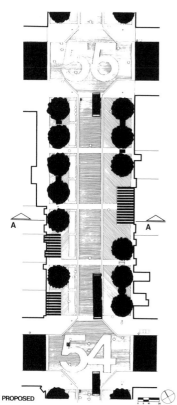

PROPOSED

(which everywhere in midtown are narrower than the original sidewalks laid out over 100 years ago for a community of four-story row houses). Trees would be planted along these new pedestrian streets and provisions made for bus lanes, offering to the harried shopper an attractive and easy alternative to the inefficient and polluting taxicab. Delivery hours would be limited, and an attempt made to consolidate delivery service, and enforce the use of smaller trucks.

In areas of highest pedestrian density at the center of the island, pedestrians and buses would have precedence, with cars and taxis shunted around the central core to the periphery of the island. Similar strategies are being implemented with increasing success in major cities around the world, and, in theory, should work well in midtown, where over 90% of the people already arrive by mass transit and over 70% of the "person miles" are travelled on foot.

Madison and Lexington Avenues, which are the narrowest north-south streets, Broadway, and 48th and 49th Streets were selected as the traffic corridors to be given over to pedestrians and buses. 48th and 49th Streets form a major development spine connecting the U.N., the north end of Grand Central Terminal, Rockefeller Center, Times Square, and the new Convention Center and passenger ship Terminal on the Hudson River waterfront.

"Movement in Midtown" offered an incremental solution to the problems of traffic reduction, goods movement, air pollution, and the need for increased open space. It was designed to be implemented in stages in conjunction with the introduction of new peripheral highways and parking garages along both the East and Hudson rivers; but it was not dependent on fancy new technologies, or the disruption of existing business districts and residential neighborhoods. It made use of existing urban space in a new way.

For a variety of reasons—and after a year of inter-agency squabbling—the Mayor decided to concentrate on implementing, as a first stage of an over-all plan, a pedestrian-transitway, or mall, on Madison Avenue. This decision left the Madison Avenue Mall, originally designed as part of a comprehensive system, open to criticism as a political

The Madison Avenue Mall, the first stage of a traffic plan for midtown Manhattan

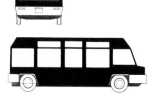

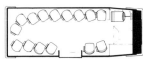

Mini-bus (or maxi-taxi) designed for the Madison Mall by Van Ginkel Associates. Buses are now called Ginkelvans.

gimmick; a one shot affair similar in kind and intent to the temporary "street closings" the Administration had been experimenting with for several years. In retrospect, the decision to do the Mall independently was a strategic error. At the time, however, it seemed that the actual construction of a major amenity would help win acceptance of the entire plan. Closing Madison Avenue to traffic at lunchtime during "Earth Week" of 1971 had been a great popular success, and a permanent mall would make the City a much more pleasant place. New Yorkers are convinced that their city is getting worse day by day, and a conspicuous improvement would make a nice change.*

The interim plan called for narrowing the Avenue to two lanes of traffic which would be used only by buses, and eventually only by mini-buses—or maxi-taxis—designed especially for the Mall by Van Ginkel Associates and inevitably dubbed Ginkelvans. Deliveries would be restricted to off hours. The additional sidewalk space created would be planted with trees and the whole avenue, street and sidewalks, attractively repaved with kiosks, benches, and bus shelters installed.

Unfortunately, the Madison Mall is not to be, at least not yet. Knowing that the Fifth Avenue Association objected to the plan, the Mayor proposed a three-month test, of the kind successfully attempted on Oxford Street in London, to see if the dire predictions of traffic congestion, reaching as far as Redding, Connecticut, would actually come true. The Fifth Avenue Association went to court, however, to prevent the City from tampering with Madison Avenue without the consent of the Board of Estimate. The Association won, and, in the subsequent Board of Estimate vote, the Mall lost, despite the strenuous efforts of the Mayor and the support of the New York Times and numerous civic groups. The decisive factor in the negative vote seems to have been the taxicab industry rather than the merchant.

If the Mall had been solely the work of outside consultants, the plan would certainly be dead. The existence of the Office of Midtown Planning and Development raises at least the possibility that the Madison Mall can be revived in the future. If the Federal Environmental Pro-

136

tection Agency's 1975 standards are enforced, far more extensive traffic restrictions will be required throughout midtown than were proposed for Madison Avenue. If the Midtown Office is still in operation, the City will have the necessary professional staff to revive the Mall concept when it is required by the Federal Government.

Our experience in New York City has led us to believe that the most effective method of helping a large city's downtown areas improve their competitive position is to create a special development office, clothed with the Mayor's authority.

Special downtown offices are a good way to see that downtown plans are carried out

The heads of these offices then have the authority to co-ordinate the activities of the city's special purpose agencies as they affect his district, both in terms of day-to-day operations and new construction and special projects. These offices are the nearest thing yet operating to the system of Little City Halls we had helped propose in 1965, which is described in the previous chapter.

The first of these offices was set up in lower Manhattan, essentially at the request of the Downtown Lower Manhattan Association. Its initial structure was devised by Donald Elliott, working with Richard Buford, its first director. When Jaquelin Robertson became the first director of the Office of Midtown Planning and Development, he added additional responsibilities and capabilities to the development office concept, with much more emphasis on urban design. Richard Weinstein later enlarged the role of the lower Manhattan office in a similar way. The downtown Brooklyn office was devised from the same pattern and other offices followed for Jamaica Center, and so on.

Alvin Toffler refers in his book *Future Shock* to what he calls the "ad-hocracy," the modern system of setting up ad-hoc organizations to achieve a specific set of goals, rather than relying on established institutions. The proliferation of these development offices is rather on an ad hoc basis, but they perform a function which would not otherwise be done.

Planners are fond of saying that planning is a continuous process, and certainly, if a project goes forward, there is no one point at which it can be said that planning has stopped and implementation has begun.

If the downtown Brooklyn planning effort had ended in 1969, very little would have taken place. Plans need to be developed further, adjusted, changed and improved in response to events. The Downtown Brooklyn Office was able to oversee the planning of the parking garage, without being caught up in the special interests of the Department of Traffic, the Department of Public Works, the Economic Development Administration, or the department store. It was also able to co-ordinate the planning of the office buildings in the urban renewal district, which are being done through the City's Economic Development Administration, and the housing on Schermerhorn Street, which is being done by the State's Urban Development Corporation.

This co-ordination has to be done by a City official. Donald Moore's Downtown Brooklyn

Sketch of proposed Madison Mall. The historic Villard Houses are at left, St. Patrick's Cathedral on the right.

Development Association is an exceptionally effective private organization, but its function is that of a civic group and a chamber of commerce, and it can't do the work of government.

No planner or urban designer can expect that every concept he devises can be carried through to a successful completion, but the special development offices created in New York provide a combined planning and implementation mechanism that makes success far more likely.

These offices also provide an organization whose primary purpose is urban design: that is, the design of the City's co-ordinative elements and public spaces, the places at ground level and the levels just above and below which are the primary matters of public concern. Such a change in the city's administrative structure can make a substantial difference to the quality of urban life.

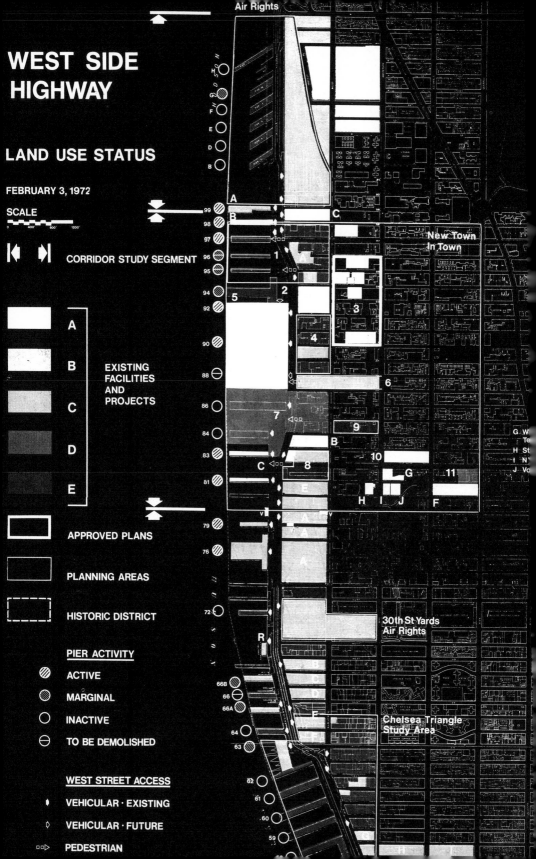

WEST SIDE HIGHWAY

LAND USE STATUS

FEBRUARY 3, 1972

SCALE

CORRIDOR STUDY SEGMENT

EXISTING
FACILITIES
AND
PROJECTS

A
B
C
D
E

APPROVED PLANS

PLANNING AREAS

HISTORIC DISTRICT

PIER ACTIVITY

ACTIVE

MARGINAL

INACTIVE

TO BE DEMOLISHED

WEST STREET ACCESS

VEHICULAR · EXISTING

VEHICULAR · FUTURE

PEDESTRIAN

Air Rights

New Town
In Town

30th St Yards
Air Rights

Chelsea Triangle
Study Area

Transportation, the urban armature

If there is anything more controversial than a new publicly-aided housing project, it is a new highway. While a community has a clear right to react to changes in a neighborhood, and to try to modify official plans, a highway represents a special situation. It would be a rare neighborhood in any urban area that could perceive a highway as an advantage, but the rights of the neighborhood have to be balanced against the needs of the city and region. After decades of highway planning that took little or no account of individual neighborhoods, the pendulum has swung in the other direction. Communities have learned to organize to defeat highway construction, and many inner-city highway plans have been immobilized by well-managed local opposition.

In some cases, these highways may well have been superfluous, or their local disadvantages were so great as to outweigh any benefits that they might confer on a larger region. There are still times when it is necessary to build a highway in a city, however; and ways have to be found to make the result politically acceptable, and as advantageous as possible to everyone who lives near the right-of-way.

One very beneficial effect of organized public opposition to highways has been that it has forced new policies on the road-building establishment. Public officials charged with building highways have traditionally kept very closely to that single purpose. They have seen themselves as road-builders, who should do their jobs as efficiently as possible. Efficiency has not included a concern for the economic and social consequences of highway construction; cost and benefit have been evaluated only on the basis of numbers of vehicles that can move from point to point.

It is well known that highways have a tremendous economic impact upon the areas in which they are built. The effect in urban areas is often negative, disrupting businesses and blighting neighborhoods. In less densely settled areas, new highways are a substantial economic stimulus: land around interchanges increases enormously in value, and whole new districts are opened up to intensive real-estate development. One sometimes hears of public officials making money illegally by buying land along highway routes that

they have learned about through inside information, but governments have not used these land
development side effects as an instrument of
public policy.

The entire Interstate system was laid out to
tie together existing population centers, and no
attention was given to the new development that
the highways were certain to stimulate.

Nor did the original planners of the Interstate system consider that there should be any
significant difference between a highway rolling
through open countryside, and one cutting
through a city, and remedial measures to correct
the effect of highways on the city have not been
part of highway plans.

It was not until the Federal Highway Act of
1970 that there were strong legal requirements
for planning highways in conjunction with other
development. In addition, the Federal Clean Air
Act of 1970 and the requirement for Environmental Impact Statements in the National Environmental Policy Act of 1969 provide some leverage
to make the highway establishment change its
ways.

The result has been the increasing use of joint
development: the planning of a highway jointly
with new buildings and other changes in environment and land use along the right of way.

**Relating highway design
to the rest of the city**

From what once appeared to be a relatively
straightforward engineering problem, highway
design has become a complex, multi-disciplinary
enterprise, involving an awesome variety of
specialists, many different governmental agencies
at Federal, State and local levels, and the participation of community groups all along the right
of way.

Back in 1968, before the new Federal legislation on highways had been drafted, Archibald
Rogers was our consultant on the "Linear City"
proposal, a joint-development project based upon
a projected Cross Brooklyn Expressway. Rogers
spent several months sorting out the jurisdic-
tions involved and their inter-relationships, the
timing of the contracts, the schedule of approvals
and so on, only to see the project vetoed by the
State Department of Transportation. The City
and Federal authorities had been in favor, but
the co-operation of all three levels of government

was necessary. State highway officials were not willing to see their control over highway design diluted by what they considered to be extraneous considerations, although they were aware that there was little likelihood that the controversial highway could be built except as a part of a larger development plan. In fact, this highway, which is badly needed, has not been built, and there is little prospect that it will be.

In 1968 we were a bit ahead of our time. Through Rogers' influence, an experimental joint development study was funded in Baltimore, and efforts were made to change the Federal legislation to make such planning mandatory. It is, of course, very difficult to assess who is responsible for major changes in a law, but the testimony co-ordinated by The American Institute of Architects, which included that of Rogers and Jaquelin Robertson, representing New York, was certainly influential.

By 1971, New York City, now backed by the Federal requirements for joint development, was ready to try highway corridor planning again, not, as it turned out for the Cross Brooklyn Expressway, but for Manhattan's West Side Highway.

This is a project of extraordinary complexity. The west side of Manhattan is already densely developed, and there is an existing highway already in operation, although it is only four lanes and the elevated portions are in bad structural condition. The right-of-way passes through some of the best-organized and most articulate communities in the City, including the West Village, home territory of Jane Jacobs. Mrs. Jacobs, the author of two highly respected books on city planning, no longer lives in Greenwich Village; but the memory of her exploits lingers on, including organizing protests that drove the Chairman of the Planning Commission out of office in the early 1960's, and caused the demapping of the Lower Manhattan Expressway in 1969.

Other problems were created when the New York State Urban Development Corporation published a plan for a redeveloped highway as the stimulus for massive new development. This document had the effect of infuriating the State Department of Transportation, whose jurisdiction

The West Side Highway Project

Community Board Boundaries

Project Study Area Boundary

Existing West Side Highway

The West Side Highway corridor borders some of the most complex and densely utilized parts of the City.

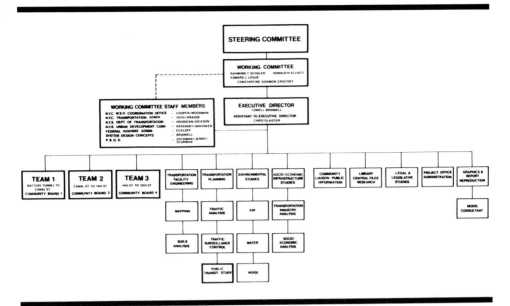

Phase I		Phase II	Phase III	Phase IV	Phase V	Public Hearings	Steering Committee Recommendations
Preliminary Alternative Designs		Selection of Program Packages	Development & Refinement of Program Packages	Evaluation of Program Packages	Preparation for Public Hearings		

Goals and Objectives	— — — — — —		
Administrative and Legal	— — — — — —	Alternative A	
Land Use and Socio-Economic Studies	— — — — — —		
Traffic Study	— — — — — —	Alternative B	Recommended
Highway Design	— — — — — —		Alternative
Public Transit	— — — — — —	Alternative C	
Air Quality Study	— — — — — —		
Noise Study	— — — — — —	Alternative D[1]	
Water Quality Study	— — — — — —		

1 One of the alternatives carried to Public Hearing is the "Do-Nothing Alternative."

was being invaded, and the Battery Park City Corporation, also a State agency, which had conflicting plans for the land-fill area at the tip of Manhattan Island. The various City agencies were also less than pleased, and the plan provoked heated discussion in the west side Community Planning Boards.

The Urban Development Corporation's plan had many good features, but the manner of its presentation was retrogressive. It is hard for planners and designers to realize that just publishing their ideas is not enough to cause every one else to swing into line. If this technique ever worked in the past, which is doubtful, it certainly doesn't work today.

As there is a serious need for a new highway, and because the Federal law now requires joint development studies, it was necessary to create a forum that would bring the decision-makers together and persuade them to agree to an orderly series of choices. The method adopted is similar in concept to the working committees used so successfully to create community participation in neighborhood planning (see chapter four) but life is considerably more complicated when this technique is applied to a highway.

A complex organization for a complex task

On the basis of a Memorandum of Understanding between the Mayor and the Governor, much of which was drafted by Alexander Cooper, the present director of the Urban Design Group, a twenty-member steering committee has been created. This committee consists of the heads of eight City agencies, six State agencies, four Community Planning Boards and two elected officials, the City Comptroller and the Borough President of Manhattan. The City agencies are the City Planning Department, the Department of Transportation, the Economic Development Administration, the Environmental Protection Administration, the Recreation and Cultural Affairs Administration, and the Offices of Lower Manhattan Development and Midtown Planning and Development.

The State agencies are the Department of Transportation, the Parks Commission, the Metropolitan Transportation Administration, the Urban Development Corporation, the Battery Park City Corporation, and the Port of New York Authority.

No Federal agencies are participants in the committee, but to the extent that the programs they administer are required, their presence is definitely felt.

To simplify matters somewhat, the steering committee has designated a working committee consisting of four members: the heads of the City Planning Commission, City Department of Transportation, State Department of Transportation, and the State Urban Development Corporation, for more direct supervision of the Project.

The executive director, and manager, of the West Side Highway Project is Lowell Bridwell, formerly the Federal Highway Administrator in Washington. The Project staff is drawn from Bridwell's firm, Systems Design Concepts, Inc., and from the staff of some of the principal consultants to the project, such as the engineers, Parsons, Brinckerhoff, Quade and Douglas. The Urban Development Corporation has provided additional staff, and six members of the Urban Design Group have been seconded to the Project. Alexander Cooper, in addition to his duties as the City's Director of Urban Design, is the director of the West Side Highway Co-ordinating Office, which is a Mayoral office that oversees the relationships between the City's agencies and the West Side Highway Project, and articulates policy for the City.

A final complication has been created by the four Community Planning Boards' refusal to accept the West Side Highway Project staff as their staff. They have insisted on hiring consultants of their own, an interesting example of the advocacy and pluralism so eloquently urged upon the planning profession by Paul Davidoff.* *See note page 88

At this writing, the committee is still considering the various alternatives put before it by the staff. The Project must steer a very narrow course between two serious dangers, on the one hand the failure to reach agreement, and, on the other, agreement to a plan that can not be implemented.

The Memorandum of Understanding provides that the Governor and Mayor can negotiate a decision of their own, in the event of the failure of the Projects committee to reach agreement. If this should happen, and if the result is unacceptable to one or more of the Community Planning Boards, or to the Borough President or Comptroller, who are both politicians elected in their own right, there is every chance that the highway will be tied up in litigation for the foreseeable future.

Preliminary estimates for the cost of building the West Side Highway are so high that the highway would not be considered practicable except for the value that can be ascribed to the land created by land-fill, or decking, depending on the alignment chosen. However, the joint development proposals being studied for the West Side Highway development corridor require

147

expenditures many times greater than for the highway itself. If the highway is to be generator of a new transit system, a freight distribution network for the west side of Manhattan, thousands of units of new housing, new parks, and so on, a way has to be found to fund these projects on something like the same time schedule as the highway itself.

Joint development also requires increased construction costs to meet Federal environmental standards, which set stringent noise and pollution standards for development in highway corridors. Long sections of the highway will probably have to be decked over and artificially ventilated.

Joint development is a device for overcoming the defects of urban planning by single purpose agencies, but the governmental context is still a series of programs each administered by an agency devoted to that single purpose.

At this time there seems to be no alternative to joint development as the means of building urban highways, but no one has yet made joint development work.

Relating transit design to the rest of the city

New underground transit systems are built far less frequently than highways; as the costs are in excess of $50-million a mile, that is not too surprising. New York, however, is in the process of constructing major extensions to its subway system, including the new Second Avenue subway line, which will run from the Bronx to the southern tip of Manhattan. Rapid transit lines, like highways, are generators of real-estate development: land around stations becomes more valuable, and new districts are opened up to more intensive development. Normally transit planning is as single purpose as highway planning; new lines are planned to serve existing populations, and not the increased number of people who will inhabit the new buildings that inevitably follow the construction of the line.

Through the good offices of the Mayor's Council on Urban Design, the City and the State's Metropolitan Transportation Administration agreed to set up a planning and design study that would relate projected new development to the design of the transit lines themselves. An inter-agency committee was created, with two State members, the Metropolitan Transportation

Outboard

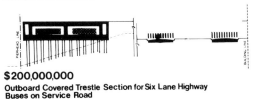

$200,000,000

Outboard Covered Trestle Section for Six Lane Highway
Buses on Service Road

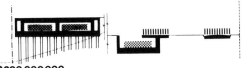

$290,000,000

Outboard Covered Trestle Section for Six Lane Highway
Plus Open Depressed Section For Transit in West Street

Inboard

$310,000,000

Inboard Covered Depressed Section for Six Lane Highway
Buses on Service Road

$270,000,000

Inboard Open Depressed Section for Six Lane Highway
Buses on Service Road

$360,000,000

Inboard Covered Depressed Section for Six Lane Highway
Transit in Depressed Section

$310,000,000

Inboard Open Depressed Section for Six Lane Highway
Transit in Depressed Section

Note:

Costs do not include R.O.W. cost, bus stations and rail conversion cost.

The above costs include the cost of the Brooklyn Tunnel Interchange and Ramps which is estimated at $60,000,000 and which is essentially the same for all the alternative sections.

▓▓▓▓▓ Mainline   ⫼⫼⫼⫼⫼ Service Road   ▒▒▒▒▒ Transit

Administration and the Transit Authority, and seven City members: the City Planning Department, the Budget Bureau, the Transportation Administration, the Housing and Development Administration, the Economic Development Administration, the Mayor's Office, and the Mayor's Council on Urban Design. The committee was

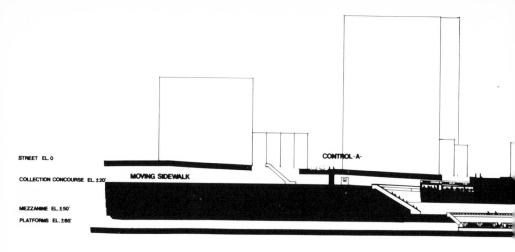

STREET EL. 0

COLLECTION CONCOURSE EL. ±20'

MOVING SIDEWALK

CONTROL·A·

MEZZANINE EL. ±50'

PLATFORMS EL. ±65'

Drawings made in the Urban Design Group to illustrate mezzanines and concourses making connections between the new Second Avenue Line and surrounding new buildings. Without such coordination, the public spaces for the new line will be built under the street, without the convenience or amenity possible through coordinated development.

called the Transit/Land-Use Working Committee. The director of the Urban Design Group served as the executive for the committee, and most of the staff was drawn from the Design Group.

The working relationship was a difficult one because the City had no actual power over the design of the lines. In order to keep the design process "free of political pressures," the City had turned over all decisions to the State's Metropolitan Transportation Administration, which is both to build and operate the lines. The engineers in charge of the project, unlike the highway builders, had not been softened up by a decade of acrimonious public hearings, and they felt that urban design suggestions would be useful only in a peripheral way.

We were therefore not able to achieve a true joint development situation in which urban designers could work directly with engineers. Instead we worked in parallel, with some informal exchange of information, and some rather stately formal presentations.

While the engineers thought that urban designers and architects are the people who choose the wall finishes in subway stations, we were concerned about the design of the routes themselves, which had already been approved by the Board of Estimate.

The Board is reported to have made its decision on this controversial set of issues in a rather unscientific way. The Metropolitan Transportation Administration had presented the proposed routes to the Board, and the Mayor had presented some modifications suggested by a staff

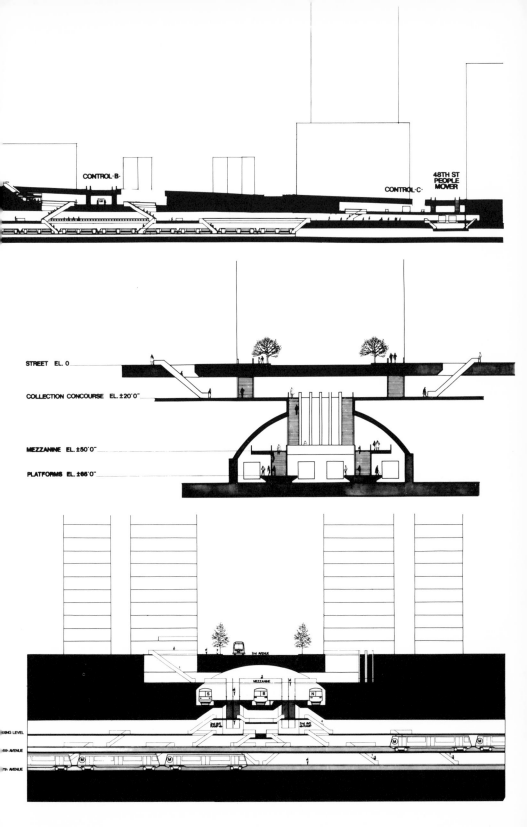

CONTROL·B·

CONTROL·C·

48TH ST
PEOPLE
MOVER

STREET EL. 0

COLLECTION CONCOURSE EL. ±20'0"

MEZZANINE EL. ±50'0"

PLATFORMS EL. ±65'0"

2nd AVENUE

MEZZANINE

S   B   N

MIXING LEVEL

6th AVENUE

7th AVENUE

review in a number of different City agencies. The Board had then added some routes in Queens and Brooklyn, which had been projected in the past but were not in the present request at all. The additional lines were included not for transportation reasons so much as to see that the residents of these boroughs received an equal share of the money being expended.

The Brooklyn routes seemed to us to be such an unsound addition that we prepared a counterproposal, and took it to all the Community Planning Boards in the Borough. Most of the community leaders were astonished to learn that the M.T.A. was actually going to build lines which had been rumored for more than fifty years. They listened carefully to our explanations that changing population patterns had made these routes ineffective, and, in general, they agreed. They did not think much of our counterproposal, however. It became clear that most of the communities affected did not want new transit lines at all; they wanted better bus service and free transfers at existing rapid transit stations.

As the Brooklyn lines had only been approved for political reasons, the lack of strong political support for them makes them a much lower priority than had originally been intended.

One function of urban design is to conceptualize issues

The engineering establishment would have gone ahead with the lines. They knew that the routes, which would cost something like half a billion dollars to build, would be of relatively small benefit to the public; but their job was to implement the decisions made by the politicians. It was also an opportunity to demonstrate efficiency; the engineering required was not difficult; and many of the necessary drawings had been in the files for years.

The politicians, thinking in general terms, were legitimately concerned that improvements in the transit system be made over as wide an area of the City as possible, and the lack of such a balance was a definite defect in the original technical proposals.

Someone else was needed to conceptualize the issues, to point out that $500-million will buy an awful lot of buses, to take the time to explain to the people most affected what the issues were, and what some of the alternatives might be.

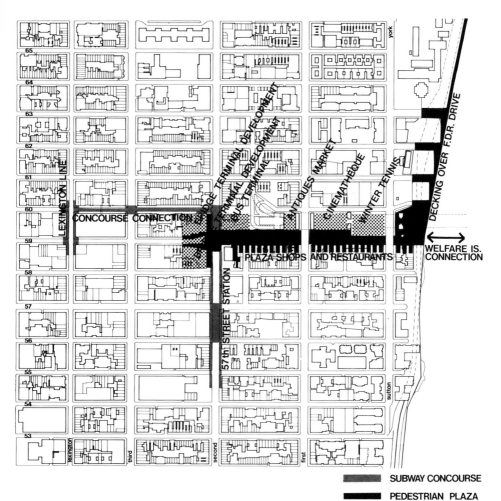

SUBWAY CONCOURSE

PEDESTRIAN PLAZA

NEW ACTIVITIES

PLAZA SHOPS

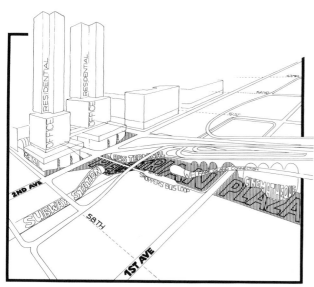

Plan co-ordinating new development anticipated to accompany the construction of the Second Avenue Subway station at 57th Street.

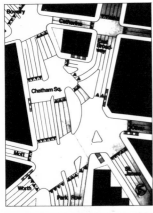

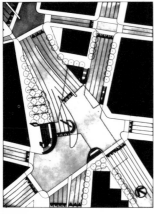

Proposal for the Chatham Square station of the Second Avenue line requires re-routing and consolidation of traffic in the Square.

Joint development studies are a good way to bridge the gap between general political considerations and technical engineering problems; to bring communities into the decision-making process, along with the over-view that the planner and urban designer can provide.

Another area in which our Transit/Land-Use studies were able to exercise considerable influence was over station locations on the Second Avenue line, which is to be built on Manhattan's east side during the next decade. In addition to providing utilization information for station locations, based on plans and studies generally not available to the M.T.A., we also suggested that some of the most heavily used stations have entrances and exits at each end of the platform rather than the center. As the Second Avenue line will be two tracks, it will not have separate express and local trains. It is therefore important that each station serve as large an area as possible, without stations being so close together that service becomes too slow. A normal platform length is six hundred feet, which is almost three blocks. With double entrances the access to the same station can be separated by as much as five blocks, greatly increasing the service area of each stop.

We also prepared detailed design and land use plans for the blocks directly around the stations, with the hope that the design of new buildings going up at roughly the same time that the stations are being constructed could be co-ordinated with the design of the stations themselves, and that city improvements, such as road widenings, bus stations and park development could also be tied into with station construction.

Some of these plans will take some very tricky co-ordination to execute, and it is not clear what the implementation mechanism will be. The Metropolitan Transportation Authority can not commit funds to a speculative plan that may or may not be done in the future, so that any unexpected delay or other failure in co-ordination means the loss of the plan.

Enough has been done, however, to demonstrate that the principle of co-ordinating transit planning with other kinds of land use and urban design plans can make a big difference to the shape of the City. Perhaps future transit lines,

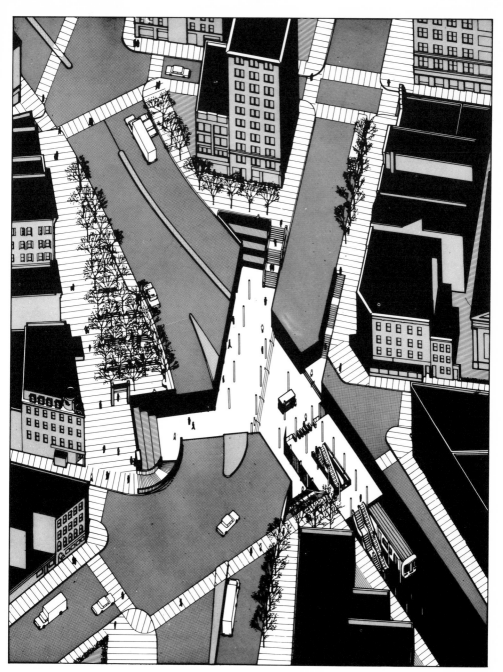

This simple and rational
plan for the Chatham Square
station mezzanine will only
be possible if the City and
the State Transportation
Authority co-ordinate their
actions precisely.

The Harlem-Park Avenue Project

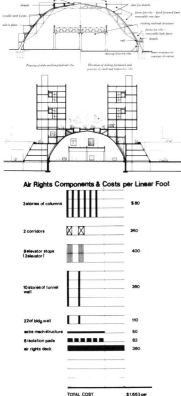

Air Rights Components & Costs per Linear Foot

3 stories of columns	|||||	$80
2 corridors	⊠ ⊠	240
8 elevator stops (2 elevator)		400
10 stories of tunnel wall		360
22 of bldg. wall		110
extra mech structure		50
8 isolation pads		63
air rights deck		360

TOTAL COST	$1,663 per linear foot
COST per SFT of RIGHT OF WAY	$12

air rights deck

The original Harlem-Park Avenue proposal was based on a concrete vault that permitted utilization of the air rights over the railway viaduct, and created protected courts and walkways where access could be controlled. Revised proposal uses more economical means to achieve a somewhat similar result.

in New York and other cities, will be carried out by a development authority that has wider powers than just building transit. Then joint development plans can be combined with joint development execution.

In talking about joint development for rapid transit lines, it is worth saying a few words about the proposal to redevelop the Park Avenue right of way of the Penn Central Railroad as it passes through Harlem on its way northward out of the City.

The original concept for this project was drawn by my colleagues, Giovanni Pasanella, Jaquelin Robertson, Richard Weinstein, Myles Weintraub and myself, before we began to work for the City. It was presented at an exhibition of the Museum of Modern Art in January of 1967. The design was what is known in the architectural trade as a "linear megastructure," not quite such a cliché at that time as it has since become. The railroad emerges from a tunnel under Park Avenue at 97th Street, and runs on an elevated viaduct through Harlem to a bridge across the Harlem River at 134th Street. We suggested that the viaduct be enclosed by a concrete vault, devised by David Geiger, the structural engineer who has invented a number of unusual new structures, including that of the United States pavilion at Expo 70 in Osaka. The vault would be strong enough to take two rows of apartment buildings, which would in turn provide relocation spaces for the people who lived in substandard housing on either side of the tracks, creating a two-block-wide development corridor.

This proposal had most of the defects that we now find so laughable in other people's plans. It was a product of "superior wisdom" planning, done without any community consultation, and exhibited at the Museum of Modern Art, the true embodiment of elitism if ever there was one. Further, the project was only feasible if it were done all at once, requiring split-second timing between numerous different agencies, none of which were used to working with each other.

Recognizing all of this, we still thought it was quite a good idea and were grateful to the museum for giving us the opportunity to develop it. The noise and dirt from the railway viaduct

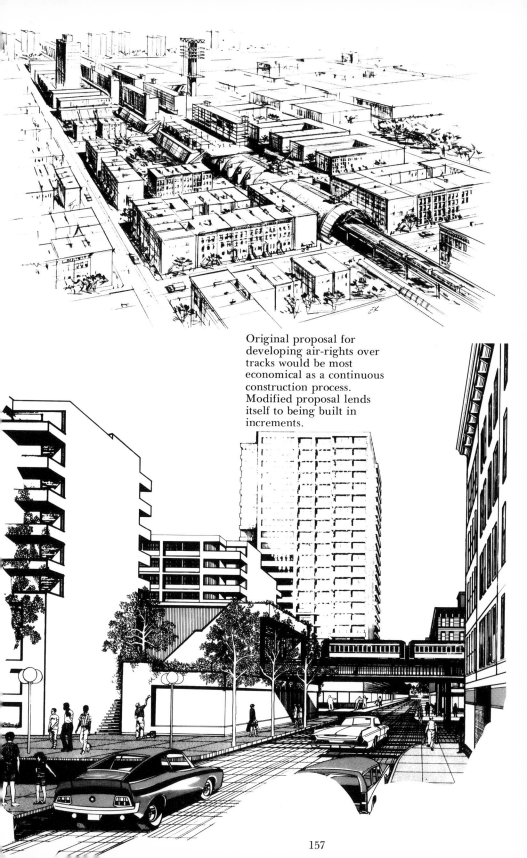

Original proposal for developing air-rights over tracks would be most economical as a continuous construction process. Modified proposal lends itself to being built in increments.

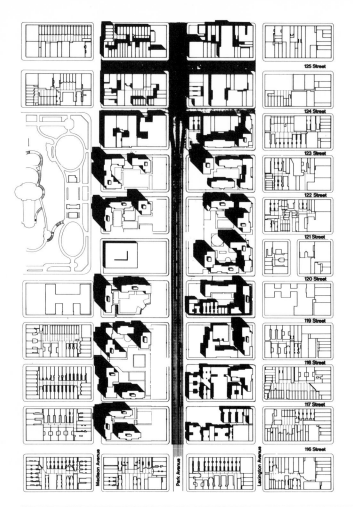

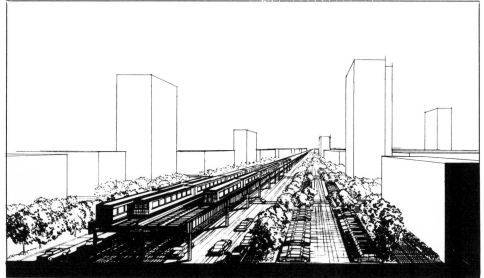

If the railway viaduct is left alone, surrounding new development will use the area nearest the tracks for parking, creating a wide, no-man's-land.

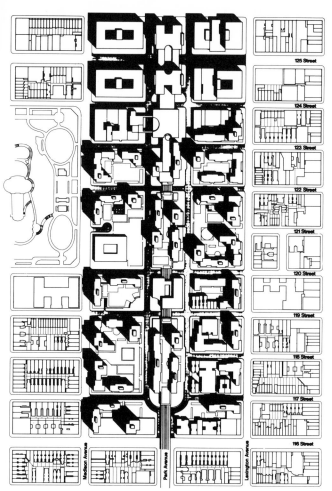

Developing the air-rights over the railway makes better use of available land, does not split up community.

were a primary cause of the deteriorated housing conditions in Harlem, and the air rights over it were a prime resource. If the cost of development of the air rights came close to the cost of purchasing and clearing land elsewhere in Harlem, it would be both a feasible and desirable project.

When we went to work for the City, we were encouraged to try to make the Park Avenue corridor proposal practicable. We put a team of urban designers, under Lauren Otis and Edwin Woodman, into the Harlem Model Cities Office, and we went through the whole apparatus of community consultation. We were also able to have some further engineering studies done by David Geiger, who, working with Ed Woodman, devised a much simpler structure that could be built in increments.

The final proposal was quite a different concept from the design that had been exhibited at the Museum of Modern Art. Instead of having a strong design character of its own, the new concept was very flexible, and could be incorporated into the plans for the different districts along the way. The plans for a pilot segment to run from 110th Street to 122nd Street were formally approved by planning councils on both sides of the right of way, and made part of the Harlem Model Cities Plan. They were also approved in principle by the City agencies like the Department of Traffic whose approval was necessary.

The problem now is funding. The enclosure of the right-of-way is not housing, nor does it come under any of the other standard categories for capital funds. While the sum of money involved is relatively small, it has never been put into the City's capital budget.

There was a time when the Federal government would have been willing to fund a showcase Model Cities project in Harlem; but, by the time we had the project together, the sources of money had dried up.

Perhaps some day the concept will capture the imagination of one of the City's political leaders. In the meantime, it has to be classed as a failure, although we still think it is a good idea.

The 48th Street Corridor

Some of what we learned by working on the Park Avenue corridor has been applied to the development plans for the 48th Street corridor in the western part of midtown Manhattan.

Although it is the back-up area for the midtown business district, the lack of rapid transit access to the blocks west of Eighth Avenue has meant that this part of the City's center is far less intensively developed than land a few steps to the east. While the area has important functions as a residential district and as the home of many useful enterprises that can not afford to pay high rent, it is potentially most valuable as the site for the orderly expansion of the midtown office and commercial district.

The alternatives would be to see the office center expand to the east side of Second Avenue or down Park Avenue South and lower Lexington Avenue, both of which would be far more destructive of existing high quality development—and far more productive of increased congestion— than an orderly planned development in the western part of midtown.

Our studies of west midtown began in response to the Port Authority's plans for a new ocean liner terminal on the Hudson River between 44th and 50th Streets. We initially retained the British architect James Stirling to work with us in planning the relationships of the terminal to the upland area around it. We also began a process of consultation with the very well-organized and sophisticated Clinton community that includes the residents of the West Forties and Fifties.

As mentioned in chapter four, the Clinton community has continued to oppose commercial development, while working with the City on the plans for the Clinton Park urban renewal area, which was meant to be part of a trade-off: a commitment to housing in Clinton in exchange for acceptance of commercial development in part of the west midtown district.

The 48th Street corridor, which had its beginnings in the Stirling study and was developed subsequently by the Urban Design Group and the Office of Midtown Planning and Development, would be the route of a cross-town transportation system connecting the ocean liner terminal to Grand Central and ultimately to the United Nations. Because this line would open up the west midtown area to development, the City originally planned to condemn the land on both sides of the right of way, and "capture" the rising property values created by the public investment in the transit system. After the 48th Street line was built, the land could be re-sold to developers at much higher prices, and the profits from this transaction could be used to provide underground truck service tunnels, parks, concourses, and other amenities, making the new development qualitatively superior to the more haphazard environment of the older parts of midtown.

Ultimately, we foresaw a three-block-wide strip of intensive commercial development running from Eighth Avenue to the Hudson River. Office buildings, hotels and large apartment houses would be set in a matrix of shopping concourses and transportation and servicing systems, providing for the orderly growth of midtown for a decade or more.

No sooner had this plan been drawn when the growth pressure in midtown began to slow down. The office market was over-built, and developers put aside their plans for new buildings. The Metropolitan Transportation Authority became dubious about the need for a conventional rapid transit system running across 48th Street, and suggested a "people-mover" instead, a technology that has not completely been invented yet. A people-mover might be a moving sidewalk, or a train that would be more flexible in its route, and easier to get on and off, than a conventional bus or subway car.

The Convention Center

The whole west midtown concept might have been shelved, if the area had not been selected as the site for a new convention center. New York City has no building capable of holding an event like a Presidential nominating convention, or the annual meeting of a really large organization. This lack represents an important deficiency in the City's economy, and the Lindsay administration had determined to remedy this situation. After careful comparative studies had been made by the Arthur D. Little Company, it became clear that the western part of midtown is the only feasible location for such a convention center.

After being chased out of a four-block site between Eleventh and Twelfth Avenues by the opposition of the local community, the Convention Center has settled in an off-shore location, just south of the liner terminal.

In order to reach the Convention Center and the liners, some sort of transportation link is clearly necessary. The construction of the link will open up blocks that are not currently suitable for intensive development. It seems only logical that the design of these blocks should be planned in advance and their construction co-ordinated with the transportation link.

Logic, of course, doesn't always carry the day. There are powerful real-estate interests who own property elsewhere, and who would rather see the zoning limits raised east of Second Avenue, for example, than west of Eighth. There is also the influence of the Clinton community. The Clinton area is not superficially very attractive, indeed it was once known as Hell's Kitchen, but its resi-

Map shows location of major proposals for western part of midtown Manhattan. Overleaf: schematic section-perspective of proposed 48th Street corridor development.

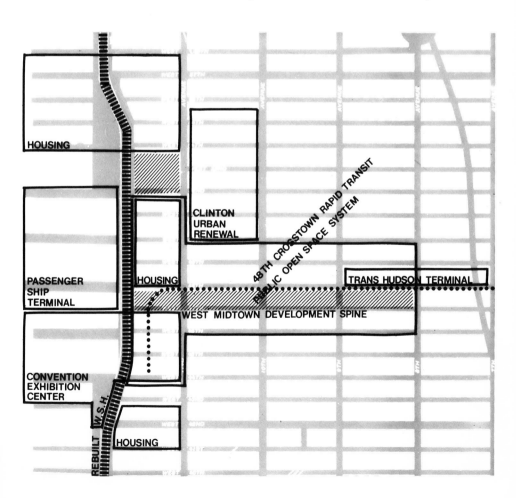

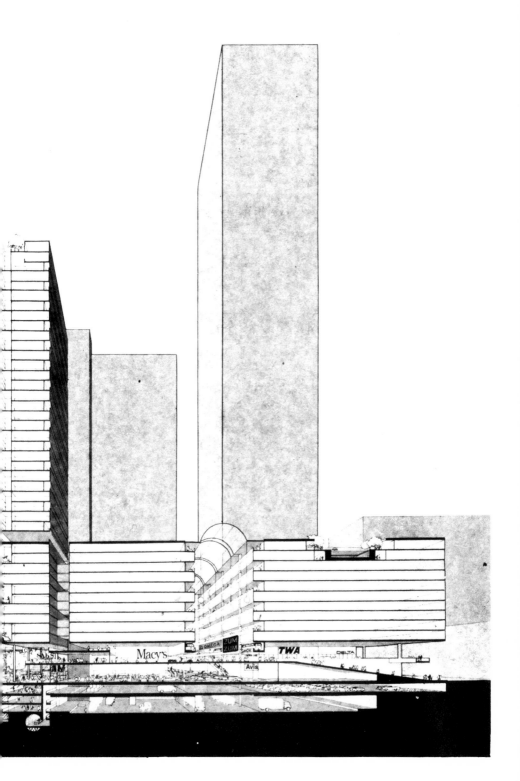

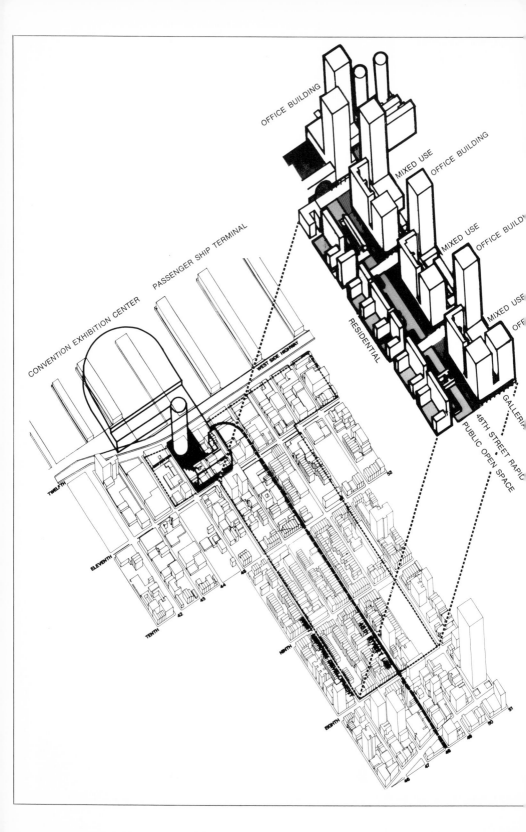

OFFICE BUILDING

MIXED USE

OFFICE BUILDING

MIXED USE

OFFICE BUILD

MIXED USE

OFF

PASSENGER SHIP TERMINAL

CONVENTION EXHIBITION CENTER

WEST SIDE HIGHWAY

RESIDENTIAL

GALLERIA

48TH STREET RAPID

PUBLIC OPEN SPACE

TWELFTH

ELEVENTH

TENTH

NINTH

EIGHTH

Co-ordinating new
development with
construction of the
48th Street crosstown line
would permit the orderly,
planned expansion of the
midtown business district,
and provide a service
infrastructure and amenities
not present in the existing
city.

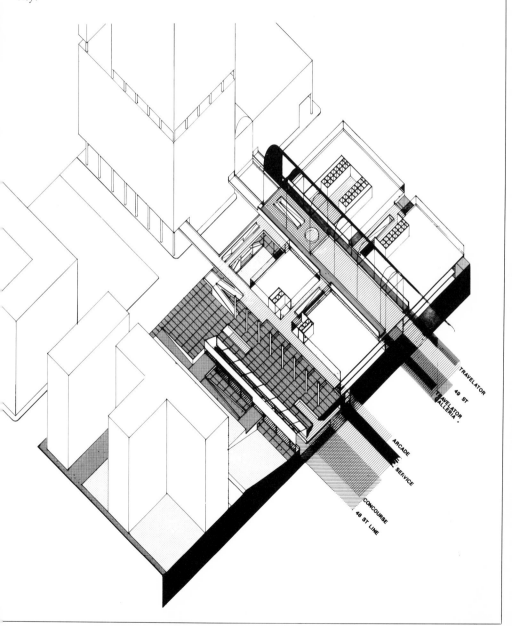

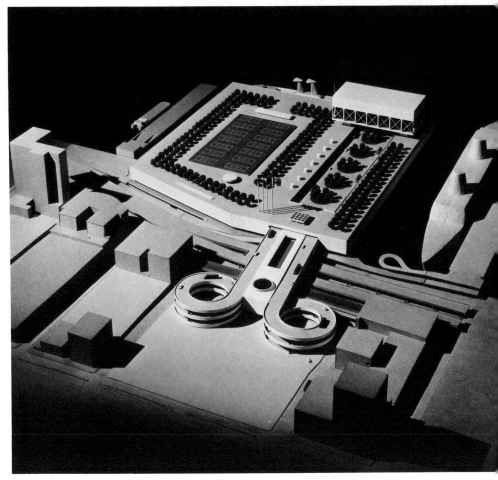

Skidmore, Owings and
Merrill's schematic
drawings for the new
convention center, planned
for the edge of the Hudson
River near the terminus
of the 48th Street line.

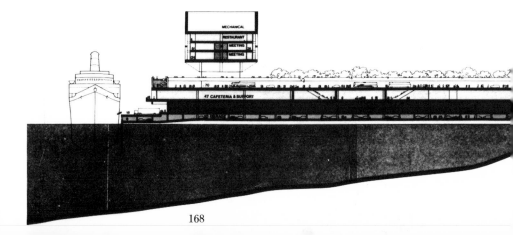

dents are attached to their homes, and would not be able to find replacements in similarly convenient locations, without paying much more rent.

Up to now, the City has taken the position that commercial expansion into Clinton is inevitable, and that expansion should therefore be a planned, high quality development. The City has recognized the interests of the Clinton community with the Clinton Park housing, but it has held that the greatest good of the greatest number meant that the 48th Street corridor plan should go ahead.

We had learned from our experience with the Park Avenue plan, that such a large-scale project had to be flexible and capable of incremental growth. We had learned from our experience with zoning districts that the part of the project that had to be designed by the City was the concourses and transportation links, not the exteriors of the office buildings or apartment houses. The liner terminal is built, and the Convention Center is in design; it seems probable that it and other elements of the 48th Street plan will be realized; but at this writing it is not a certainty.

While transportation systems are clearly one of the most powerful means of changing the design of the city, we have not yet invented the institutions that will make such changes purposive rather than accidental. The plans shown in this chapter have been created, to some extent, out of context. The development corporations or other agencies that could build them do not yet exist. We expect the development around the West Side Highway, the Second Avenue Line, and in west midtown to embody more urban design and planning considerations, after more community consultation, than such projects have done in the past; but much work still needs to be done before transportation programs can be used to their full potential as generators of city design.

Needed: a joint-development agency to build joint-development projects

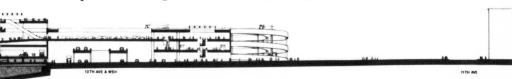

12TH AVE & WSH

11TH AVE

Photo-montage shows west
midtown development.
Clinton Housing, and other
residential projects are at
left; at right, the 48th
Street corridor and the
convention center.

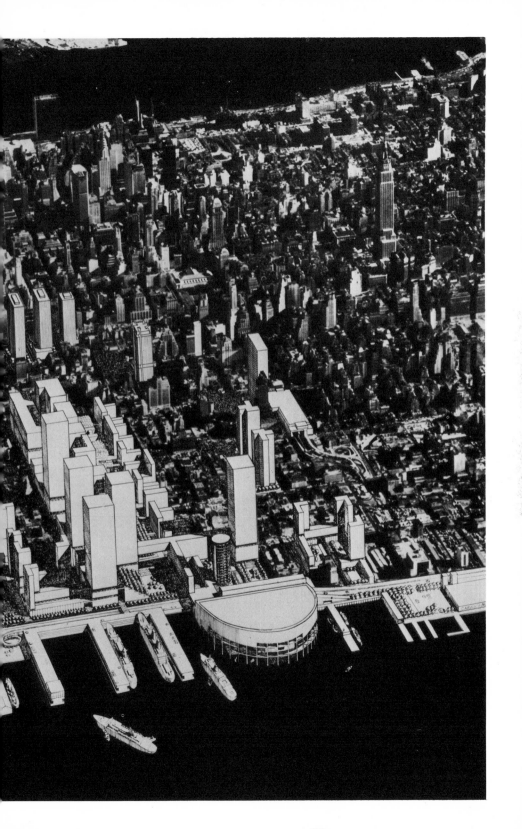

7

Design
review
and
environmental
quality

The special zoning regulations for the Theater District, and several of the subsequent special zoning districts, were created in response to specific actions taken by real estate developers.

As planning and urban design become more sophisticated, it should be possible to anticipate major land use developments and changes well in advance; but a certain amount of adaptive response will always be necessary as long as we live in a period of accelerated economic and social change.

Design review: needed, a consistent, but adaptive, response

What is needed is a response mechanism that is not so rigid as to stifle innovation and constructive change and at the same time does not succumb to the "Henny-Penny Effect:" loud cries that the sky is falling, and the end of all planning principles is at hand.

Planning authorities always have the ability to say yes or no, but they often find themselves in the dilemma of wishing to approve something in principle, but not liking certain features of the proposal. In order to make constructive suggestions, it is necessary to have a staff that is able to review the design of major projects as they come up for approval. This design review process also functions as a screening mechanism to identify major policy issues where changes in the law or in administrative practice will be necessary.

New York City has no formal design review process for private construction, although every building on public property must be reviewed by the City's Art Commission. The 1961 zoning resolution was so tightly drawn, however, that almost every major project in the central area has required either a discretionary special permit or some kind of minor modification of map or text. While deliberating over such special situations, the Planning Commission is in a position to make some suggestions.

The most important thing to remember about design review is that due process must always be observed, and the review procedure should follow clearly explicable principles and standards.

The drawings opposite, produced by the Office of Midtown Planning and Development, are part of the clear record, built up during a sequence of meetings, of what the planning authorities thought represented the most desirable alterna-

174

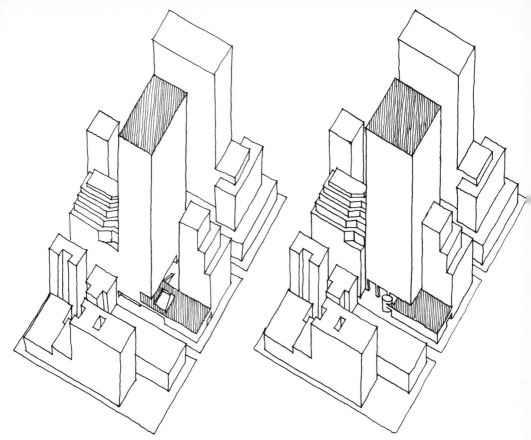

tives. With a record like this, it is possible to show that, while the choices under consideration were somewhat subjective, the decision was not made in an arbitrary manner.

Observing due process also means being consistent. It would clearly be wrong for a Planning Commission to make an exception for one developer that it would not make for another, nor should there be a situation where the developer has no alternative but to comply with the design modifications suggested by the authorities. There should be an underlying set of rules for every district which permits a developer to build "by right."

If the developer initiates a request, however, and the zoning would permit him to do something in any case, the Planning Commission does have the right to suggest modifications that relate to the subject of the special permit. If the planning authorities are being asked to make changes in the zoning which will have a permanent, general application, they can create new requirements which relate to the changes.

Two drawings from a series documenting discussions with a developer. The drawing at left shows how the building actually was constructed. The developer provided a public park on top of the low structure, in return for zoning concessions.

Richard Weinstein,
director of the Office of
Lower Manhattan
Development, describing
the galleria in the new 100
William Street Building for
Mayor Lindsay and
members of the press.
Architects are Davis, Brody
and Associates. Drawings
show exterior of building,
and position of galleria.

In the case of the special zoning districts, developers' requests set off comprehensive changes that have the effect of diminishing the need for design review in the future. In other instances, a situation created by a developer has led to text changes in the zoning whose application is not confined to a particular district. A good example is the legislation authorizing bonuses in floor area for covered pedestrian spaces —galleries—which may be substituted for plazas. The new building at 100 William Street (at left) is an application of this provision.

Over a period of time, a relatively objective format has been developed for design review studies, which specifies the points of interests to the City, without trying to dictate the architectural details of the buildings. Some examples of the format that has been devised are shown on pages 178 and 179.

The ability of planning authorities to respond to proposals flexibly, by making counter suggestions instead of saying yes or no, is of enormous importance. Of course, if the future were predictable, preferred alternatives could be specified in advance and design review would be unnecessary. In the absence of a crystal ball, a sophisticated design review procedure makes all the difference between a successful planning process and an impotent one.

Unfortunately, design review has all the defects of discretionary zoning that were discussed in chapter two. The public does not always trust government officials, and the developer does not wish to be in doubt about his building for several months while his "front end costs" continue to mount up.

There is therefore continuing pressure to codify standards in advance of development. The guide to Planned Unit Development produced by The Urban Design Group in 1968 is an early example of such a set of standards (page 38). In addition, the growing concern about environmental quality has made it necessary to try to define what "quality" is. A series of proposals for zoning changes was drawn up by New York's Urban Design Council (which is part of the Mayor's Office) and published under the title "Housing Quality, A Program for Zoning Re-

View North from the Main Lobby of the McGraw-Hill Building

An Urban Design Group proposal to Rockefeller Center–McGraw Hill to build a large galleria space was not accepted, but one has been built in the Rockefeller Center building just to the south.

Housing Quality Study: objectifying what is meant by good design

form." This study represents a long step towards the goal of replacing design review with a flexible system of standards that has been codified and published in advance of the design of individual buildings, and is generally applicable throughout the city.

As mentioned in chapter two, New York City's Comprehensive Zoning Revision of 1961 had a built-in design bias in favor of towers surrounded by open space. The provisions creating these towers were introduced as a corrective to the dark courts and light wells that characterized the old, 1916, zoning; but the changes gave rise to new problems, particularly in residential areas.

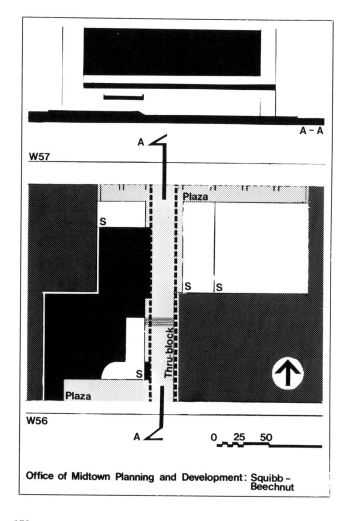

Office of Midtown Planning and Development: Squibb – Beechnut

The minimum standards written into the zoning became the specification of a new residential building type: a tower which was two or three times as tall as the neighboring buildings, surrounded by open space that was seldom pleasant, often dangerous, and, in low density districts, almost invariably filled with parked cars. The open areas break the continuity of the street facade, and the tall towers frequently throw nearby buildings into shade for much of the day. The zoning takes little account of differences in neighborhood and changes in topography; and, because of the restrictive nature of the regulations, the same stereotypes are repeated all over the City.

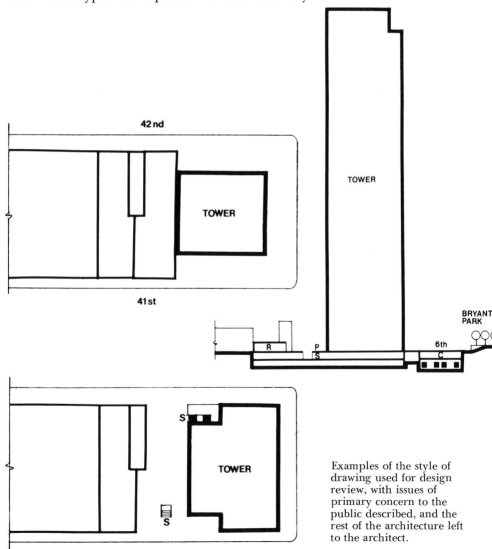

Examples of the style of drawing used for design review, with issues of primary concern to the public described, and the rest of the architecture left to the architect.

179

These new apartment towers have become very unpopular, a prime cause of the community resistance to new building projects encountered almost everywhere in New York. Not only do the neighbors object; so do the tenants. People are beginning to suspect that the tall building is not a suitable type of apartment house for anyone but the well-to-do, who can afford doormen, elevator attendants and the service staff necessary to keep the building secure and well-maintained. It also helps if the tenants can afford to escape to the country on week ends.

Tall apartment houses are not popular with developers either. It is true that high floors command premium rents, at least until the building is surrounded by other towers. But this kind of high-rise building, with its relatively small floors, is very expensive to build; and the open space and setback regulations are so restrictive that many developers have found themselves stuck with sites that could have been developed under the old regulations, but don't seem to be an economic proposition under the new law.

One solution, much advocated by developers, is to increase the zoned density all over the City. This move would make building more profitable for the developer, until the land prices had risen to take account of the change. All the other criticized factors of the 1961 zoning would simply be made even less acceptable.

If there is to be no increase in density, it is not possible to use new incentive provisions similar to those for plazas or covered pedestrian spaces, or like those in use in the special districts.

Instead, the Urban Design Council has accepted the existing residential zones and their mapped density as being based on sound planning principles, but suggests scrapping all the technical aspects of residential zoning controls that are not mandated by other sets of regulations, like the Building Code and the Multiple Dwelling Law.

In place of setback lines or open space ratios, the developer, and his architect, would elect to include certain design elements in their building from a list specified in a comprehensive zoning amendment. The use of these elements would be rewarded by a point system also specified in the law. A building which had a high enough score on

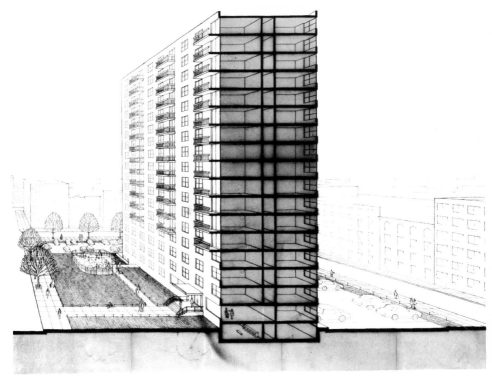

Above, the conventional New York apartment house takes a form virtually dictated by the zoning. The Housing Quality Study suggest alternatives, such as the building below, which the zoning does not now permit.

	MAXIMUM VALUE	
NEIGHBORHOOD IMPACT	Built Up	Non Built Up
1. Street wall setback*	4.55	n.a.**
2. Sunlight in open space*	3.60	4.70
3. Length of street wall*	3.60	7.55
4. Shadow on buildings*	3.05	5.40
5. Height of street wall*	3.05	n.a.
6. Street trees*	2.85	4.15
7. Height of building*	2.15	n.a.
8. Transparency ratio at ground floor*	2.15	3.20
	25.00	25.00

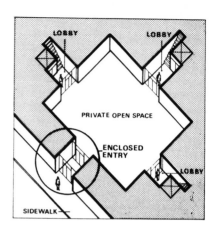

RECREATION SPACE	
1. Type and size*	8.50
2. Winter sun	5.00
3. Landscaping	2.75
4. Covered parking	2.65
5. Visibility of parking*	2.65
6. Trees*	2.45
7. Seating	1.00
	25.00

SECURITY AND SAFETY	
1. Vis. from public space to elevator door or general circulation stair	3.90
2. Vis. of priv. outdoor space from lobby*	3.90
3. Surveillance from large apartments	3.30
4. No. of apts. serviced by lobby	2.90
5. Vis. of parking from exit point*	2.25
6. Vis. of parking area from lobby	2.20
7. Distance from elevator to apt.*	1.85
8. Road separation*	1.80
9. Vis. from elevator door or general circulation stair to apartment door*	1.80
10. Visibility of mail room	1.10
	25.00

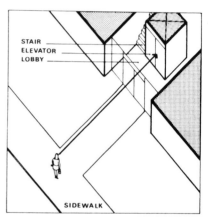

APARTMENTS	
1. Size of apartment*	3.75
2. Sunlight in apartment*	3.20
3. Window size*	3.20
4. Visual privacy--apt. to apt.*	3.20
5. Visual privacy--street to apt.	1.75
6. Balconies	1.70
7. Daylight in hallways	1.50
8. Distance from parking to garage exit*	1.50
9. Daylight in kitchen	1.50
10. Pram and bicycle storage	1.30
11. Waste storage facilities*	1.20
12. Garbage pickup facilities	1.20
	25.00

*Minimum compliance levels established

**n.a.--not applicable

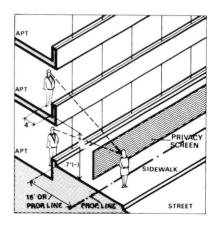

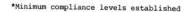

Putting an objective value to design quality: the list of possible housing quality points that a developer could obtain, and which would permit him to build to the maximum density. Drawings illustrate examples of the security and safety category.

this scale of quality points would be permitted to attain the highest floor area scheduled for that particular zoning district. Buildings whose design received a lower score would be proportionately smaller.

There would be more possible quality design elements than any one building would be expected to include, thus recognizing that design is always a series of choices, that circumstances alter cases, and you can't win 'em all: sometimes one objective can be achieved only at the expense of another. The architect would be able to choose appropriate design elements in relation to the existing neighborhood, the shape of the site, the topography, and so forth, instead of adapting the needs of his client to a single rigid stereotype.

The Design Coucil has delineated four categories of elements that are rewarded with points for design quality: they respond to criteria for Neighborhood Impact, Recreation Space, Security and Safety, and Apartment Design.

The scoring system is set up in such a way that the developer must achieve a minimum distribution of points among the four categories. A list of all the criteria, and some representative examples, are shown opposite.

The whole design quality system is the product of an exhaustive, two-year study that included the question of building costs. It is expected that the developer will be able to balance increased costs caused by some of the elements he elects, by savings created by not having to comply with some of the old regulations, and by the increased feasibility of building on many sites that were not economic before.

The new regulations would be administered in the same way as the present law, the provisions would be available by right, subject to approval by the Building Department. There would be no discretionary rulings by the Planning Commission and no individual special permits with their attendant public hearings.

The effect of this zoning amendment would be to bring the benefits of urban design policies to neighborhoods that are neither part of high intensity business districts nor in need of extensive urban renewal. It is also a principle capable of considerable extension and further development.

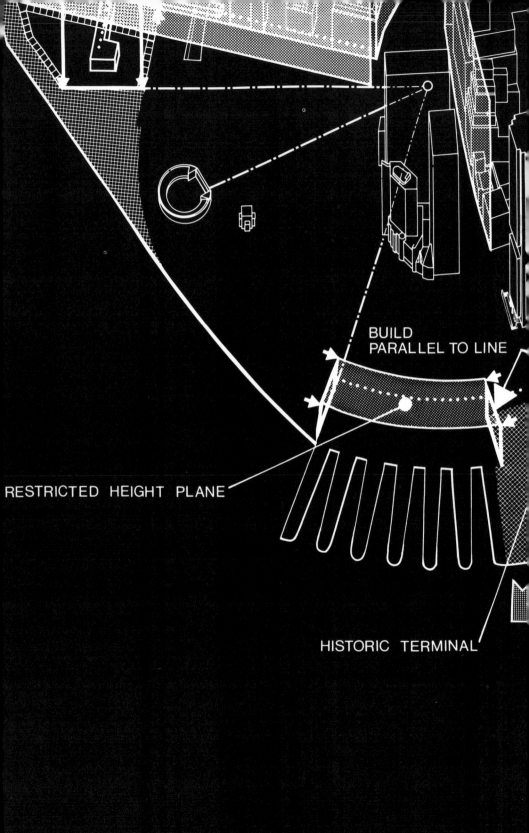

BUILD
PARALLEL TO LINE

RESTRICTED HEIGHT PLANE

HISTORIC TERMINAL

S.E. CORNER

8

Urban
design,
a new
profession

Urban designers design cities, not just the buildings

What is the difference between an urban designer and an urban planner, or between an urban designer and an architect? We were forced to consider these definitions quite seriously in New York, because we were creating a new institution and the public employees' union and the City's personnel department required that the new urban design jobs we proposed be established under civil service regulations, with the appointments made on the basis of performance on examinations.

A city planner, it seemed to us, was someone who was primarily concerned with the allocation of resources according to projections of future need. Allocating funds for a capital budget is a series of planning decisions, because it involves determinations of need for, as an example, a new school in a particular district, and balancing off that need against that of other areas.

Architects, on the other hand, design buildings. They prepare a set of contract documents so that the building, let us say a school, can be constructed, and they take legal responsibility for the process.

There is a substantial middle ground between these professions, and each has some claim to it, but neither fills it very well.

Planners tend to regard land use as an allocation of resources problem, parcelling out land, for zoning purposes, without much knowledge of its three-dimensional characteristics, or the nature of the building that may be placed on it in the future. The result is that most zoning ordinances and official land use plans produce stereotyped and unimaginative buildings.

Land use planning would clearly be improved if it involved someone who understands three-dimensional design.

A good architect will do all he can to relate the building he is designing to its surroundings, but he has no control over what happens off the property he has been hired to consider. If you visit New Haven, Connecticut, you will see some of the best recent work of American architects, both at Yale and in the surrounding urban areas, but the city is not correspondingly improved.

Someone is needed to design the city, not just the buildings.

The civil service establishment accepted this argument that there was a need for someone who could be called an urban designer. The next questions were: How could such a person be trained, and how could you judge his qualifications?

We decided that, as a practical matter, only architectural education offered any systematic training in three-dimensional design, although we did leave an opportunity for the examiners to decide that a planning degree from a school with a heavy emphasis on studio work, or qualifications as a landscape architect, or even in operations research or decision-making theory, might be considered an equivalent.

At the same time it was not necessary for an urban designer to possess the detailed knowledge of building codes required for the City's architect titles, although registration as an architect would clearly be desirable for the senior urban designer titles.

The civil service system is a mixed blessing. It does put the brakes on unqualified people being appointed for political reasons, but it tends to encourage the advancement of people of mediocre ability, who "know the ropes" and whose primary objective is job security.

The most obvious requirement for a successful civil service is the ability to attract good people, which depends on the nature of the City's leadership and the work to be done, as well as the working conditions; but the civil service exam is also highly important, if the right people are to be qualified and promoted. We were very fortunate in establishing the Urban Design Group to find a great many highly qualified and dedicated people, who were willing to work long hours and put up with the frustrations and resistance to change of large governmental organizations.

During the first two years of the Design Group's existence, we were permitted to appoint people provisionally to civil service lines, without an examination. Each new arrival, however, was selected in accordance with job specifications that had been written at the time the urban design titles were established. These outlined a whole "banana republic" of ranks: junior urban designer, assistant urban designer, urban designer, senior

Choosing urban designers under civil service regulations

urban designer, and principal urban designer. The educational and experience qualifications for each title were clearly specified.

On the other hand, we had turned away many applicants who might appear to be qualified on paper because they did not show enough evidence of design ability in their portfolios, did not seem to understand what we were trying to do, or lacked the self-assurance and entrepreneurial spirit needed to function in an environment where lines of authority were blurred and the task at hand had a way of constantly redefining itself.

How to design an examination that would take such elusive qualities into account, and would still be generally recognized as fair, could in fact survive an appeal to the Civil Service Board or a court case that might be brought by a disgruntled examinee?

We found that the people in charge of administering the civil service system were very anxious to do a good job. If we were willing to accept their regulations, they were willing to listen to suggestions about the nature of the examination and the choice of the examiners.

We found that there was a civil service procedure called a training and experience examination, in which candidates could bring a portfolio of work to be evaluated by a panel of examiners. There was also a procedure called a technical oral examination, in which examiners could ask questions directly of the candidates, and there could be a give and take discussion, provided that the same questions were asked of all candidates for a given civil service title.

In the end we achieved quite a successful examination process using a combination of these two techniques, and enormous amounts of the time of the first two examiners, George Dudley, the chairman of the New York State Council on Architecture, and George Lewis, the executive director of the New York Chapter of the American Institute of Architects.

Subsequent examinations have followed the same general pattern, thanks to the dedication of the people who have served as examiners and the civil service personnel, who have accepted a procedure that is much more cumbersome and time-consuming than a written examination.

The civil service exam was just one aspect of an effort we pursued continuously to institutionalize urban design as a function of the city government. The urban design titles should not become the description of an architect who did not have to know as much about building construction as a civil servant on an architect title and who was available to do odd jobs where "beautification" was required.

No concept could be more misleading than the idea that cities can be "beautified" without coming to grips with their fundamental problems; and no concept seems to die harder. We had to exercise continual vigilance to make sure that urban designers were on the scene when the real design decisions were being made.

I had a continuing bureaucratic struggle within the City Planning Department to preserve an Urban Design Group with institutional responsibility for important issues, rather than urban designers dispersed throughout the agency. My colleagues in the Mayor's development offices had to fight for design control over projects in their areas of responsibility against established agencies who were not used to thinking in urban design terms, and who did not like to see their turf invaded.

As mentioned at the beginning of this book, we did find it impossible to centralize urban design functions in a single office, as the Paley Commission had originally recommended. What works against such centralization is the basic principle that bureaucrats prefer to take advice from people who work directly for them.

As a counterforce, we evolved what might be called "the crab-grass response," sending out runners and spreading in all directions. We encouraged members of the Urban Design Group to take responsible jobs in other parts of the City Planning Department and in other agencies, where they could take root and gain control over decisions that involved important design issues.

My continued concern with the institutional aspects of urban design was a primary reason for my going to the City College to set up their Graduate Program in Urban Design.

A graduate program to recruit and train urban designers

From the City's point of view, this graduate program functions as both a nation-wide talent search, and as a means of giving advanced training to people already employed by the City.

Every year, ten graduates of schools of architecture are selected and, instead of the studio course that is a feature of most architectural and urban design education, they are given a part-time job working for the City. The work program is organized to take the place of studio work, and the student is paid for what he does, and receives some academic credit for it. In addition, the graduate students receive an intensive education in the context of urban design: law, public administration, real estate, the sociology of cities, environmental psychology, as well as theories and case studies of urban design. This program leads to a Master of Urban Planning (Urban Design) degree after one year.

Another ten people, with more advanced qualifications, work towards their Master's degree while employed full time as urban designers, many of them working for the City. They take the same courses as their colleagues in the regular program, but substitute a major research project for the academically supervised work experience.

We expect these graduates to do what their predecessors have done in the work described in this book: transfer their design skills from buildings to the city as a whole. The architect is not only a person who designs things on paper but the organizer of an intricate process involving many other professionals during the design stage, as well as the complexities of the building itself.

We see the urban designer working with other professionals on the design of cities, in the same way as the architect works with other professionals in the design of buildings. Needless to add, many of those who have been the *de facto* designers of cities are not necessarily willing to relinquish their role. But the architect, by training and temperament, is a person who is willing to make decisions, and an urban designer is an architect who has acquired the knowledge to make effective decisions about the design of cities. In the end, power tends to gravitate towards those who are both willing to use it, and able to use it well.

Answers for questions . . . Of course, despite the record of urban design in New York City and a few other places, the role of the urban designer is still to some extent a prediction. I once heard an urban designer defined as someone who knew the answers to a lot of questions that no one is asking.

People are starting to ask, however. Community demands for new housing that remains part of the neighborhood rather than obliterating it, Federal regulations requiring environmental impact statements, the trend towards joint development for major transportation projects: all are requirements for urban design.

. . . That people are just starting to ask.

On the other side of the table, the demonstrated success of urban design concepts like special zoning districts has awakened real-estate interests to the fact that there are things that can be done with the co-operation of government that would not be possible for the entrepreneur on his own. Another favorable circumstance for urban design is that there is more "patient money" around. Changing tax laws and other business conditions are making it more profitable to hold new developments, rather than selling them as soon as they are rented, or as soon as a maximum depreciation has been achieved for tax purposes. There is quite a difference in what a developer expects from a project if he plans to hold it rather than sell it off immediately.

The future of the urban designer lies with those governmental authorities that have the power to make large scale decisions about the environment, and in those businesses and industries whose activities have a big impact on our physical surroundings.

To put it another way, the same institutions that have been the "bad guys" in the design of cities have the greatest capacity to be the "good guys."

Such a transformation almost certainly has to begin at the top. It is impossible to exaggerate the importance of Mayor Lindsay or Donald Elliott in changing New York City's design policies, or the importance of Governor Rockefeller or Edward Logue's role in achieving high quality buildings for the New York State Urban Development Corporation. The success of day-to-day activities depends on the people doing the work, but major innovations are almost impossible in large institutions unless the leadership is in favor of change.

If the heads of major insurance companies were to make some urban design criteria the conditions for giving permanent financing, they could change the face of cities all over the nation.

Civic action by business groups and citizen groups also can make a major difference. The Downtown Lower Manhattan Association and the Downtown Brooklyn Development Association, to name only two, have been very important in both generating urban design ideas and seeing that these ideas received the proper attention from those in power. The Urban Design Council was created to help promote urban design in New York and has been enormously helpful. Groups like the Twin Parks Association have been indispensable in carrying out neighborhood renewal plans.

In the end, better urban design will be achieved by a partnership between private investment and government, and between the design professional and the concerned decision-maker in either private or public life.

The experiences described in this book represent a sample of what urban design can accomplish, but much remains to be learned, and much remains to be done.

Urban design:
a process and
a partnership

Acknowledgments

This book owes a great deal to the clarity and organizational ability of Jan V. White, the graphic designer, and to the perceptive editing of Jeanne M. Davern. I also wish to thank Patricia White for retyping the manuscript, and Annette Netburn for final proof reading.

In addition, I owe a considerable debt of appreciation to my colleagues, Jaquelin Robertson and Richard Weinstein, who read and commented upon the many drafts of this book. Like the work shown on these pages, which is the product of many hands, the theoretical formulations that we have drawn from the work have been thought out among the three of us, and it is hard to know where one man's ideas leave off and another's begin.

Having said that the work shown in these pages is very much a group effort, I should like to make an effort to assign some responsibility and credit, at least for the people who did the technical work. It would be impossible to list all the people, in all the agencies and private organizations, that have contributed in some way.

The original Twin Parks plan and the Park Avenue—Harlem project were done between 1965 and 1967, before the formation of the Urban Design Group. From April 1967 until approximately July, 1969, the Urban Design Group was run jointly by the four principal urban designers: myself, Jaquelin Robertson, Richard Weinstein and Myles Weintraub. Subsequently, the Office of Midtown Planning and Development and the Office of Lower Manhattan Development became the place where urban design work was done relating to these localities. Richard Weinstein succeeded Richard Buford as director of the Office of Lower Manhattan Development, and his deputies were, successively, Arthur Wrubel, Edgar Lampert, and Terry Williams. Jaquelin Robertson was the first director of the Office of Midtown Planning and Development. His deputy director was William Bardel, who succeeded Mr. Robertson as director in early 1973. Lauren Otis, who had been director of design, then became the deputy director.

I was the director of the Urban Design Group from 1969 to the fall of 1971, when I was succeeded by Alexander Cooper. Richard Rosan went in 1970 to the newly-created Office of Downtown Brooklyn Development, of which he was first director of design and then director.

Work done prior to establishment of Urban Design Group:

Original Twin Parks Plan: (in alphabetical order) Jonathan Barnett, Giovanni Pasanella, Jaquelin Robertson, Richard Weinstein, Myles Weintraub; assisted by Lucinda Cisler, Etel Kramer, Heidi Konwalinka

Park Avenue—Harlem Plan: (in alphabetical order) Jonathan Barnett, Jaquelin Robertson, Giovanni Pasanella, Richard Weinstein, Myles Weintraub; assisted by Benjamin Mendelsund, George Terrien, Paul Wang; structural consultant, David Geiger; mechanical and electrical systems consultant, Michael Kodaras; construction consultant, Edward Friedman

Work done in the Urban Design Group up to mid-1969:

Theater District: Richard Weinstein, Jaquelin Robertson, Jonathan Barnett, Myles Weintraub; Norman Marcus, Counsel to the City Planning Commission; Richard Steyert, economics consultant; Sean Sculley

Lincoln Square District: Richard Weinstein, Jaquelin Robertson, Rachel Ramati; Norman Marcus, Counsel to the City Planning Commission; Marilyn Groves, Commissioner Harmon Goldstone; Richard Steyert, economics consultant

Planned Unit Development: Michael Dobbins, Jonathan Barnett; Frank Rogers, Gregory Matviak; Millard Humstone, Samuel Joroff

Coney Island Plan: Alexander Cooper, Heidi Konwalinka

West Midtown Plan: Jaquelin Robertson, Ajzyk Jagoda, Lauren Otis, John Turnbull, Rumy Shroff, Alexander Caragonne, Terry Williams

Downtown Brooklyn Plan: Jonathan Barnett, Richard Rosan; Vincent P. Ponte, planning consultant; Karl DuPuy, Joan Franklin, Peter Woll, Jung Ling Wang, Mithoo Baxter

Park Avenue—Harlem Plan: Lauren Otis and Edwin Woodman; Frank Rogers, Joseph Black, Joyce Saginaw, Richard Nettey, Victor Wilbekin

Work done in the Urban Design Group from 1969 through 1973:

Transit/Land-Use Working Committee: Jonathan Barnett, executive director; Edwin Woodman, Karl DuPuy, deputy directors; Raymond Curran, John Davis, Martin Dorf, Stanton Eckstut, Mark Mutchnik, Merrill Pasco, Bruce Prince, Frank Rogers. From 1971: Alexander Cooper, executive director; Stanton Eckstut, deputy director; Daniel Brown, James Castelluzzo, Martin Dorf, Marjorie Myhill, Merry Neisner, Eva Olenmark, Michael Parley, Jeremy Walsh.

West Side Highway Project: Alexander Cooper, director, West Side Highway Co-ordination Office; Edwin Woodman, deputy director; Robert Heller, assistant to the Mayor: Allane Baerson, Martin Dorf, Celesta Fitzgerald, Eliot Lerman, Peter Pfeffer, Barry Sulam.

Housing Quality Study: Alexander Cooper, executive director, Mayor's Council on Urban Design: project directors: Michael Kwartler, Charles Reiss: Anna Bogusz, Linda Deutsch, Mary Ellen Ross, Laura West; Pares Bhattacharji, Jonah Cohen, Howard Forman, Ajzyk Jagoda, Michael Parley, Jeremy Walsh. Prior studies by Raeburn Chapman and Rachel Ramati.

Work done in the Office of Downtown Brooklyn Development from 1969:

Atlantic Ave. Zoning District: Richard Rosan, Robin Burns, June Blanc

Brooklyn Center Project: D. Kenneth Patton, Economic Development Administrator; Paul Levine, Richard Rosan.

Special Zoning District: Richard Rosan, Robin Burns, Pares Bhattacharji

Fulton Street Mall: Hardy Adasko, June Blanc, Douglas Brooks, David Hirsch Janine Kahane

Livingston-Bond Garage: Richard Rosan, Robin Burns, Reed Coles, Richard Mandel

Schermerhorn St. Mezzanine: Richard Rosan, Felix Martorano, Reed Coles, Janine Kahane, Vickie Pei, Robert Votavi

Schermerhorn Street Urban Renewal Plan: Richard Rosan; Robert Hazen and William Hayden of the New York State Urban Development Corporation; Barry Zeligson; Vickie Pei, Joan Wallick

Work done in the Office of Lower Manhattan Development from 1969:

Greenwich Street District: Richard Weinstein, Edgar Lampert, Arie Shafer, John West, Pares Bhattacharji, Also: Donald Elliott, chairman of the City Planning Commission, Norman Marcus, counsel to the Planning Commission, Alfred Schimmel of the City Planning Department. Consultants: Haines, Lundberg & Waehler: Jack Smith and Millard Humstone.

One Hundred William Street (design review): Richard Weinstein, Edgar Lampert.

South Street Seaport Air Rights Transfer: Richard Weinstein, Edgar Lampert, Terry Williams, Richard Baiter, Kenneth Halpern, Stephen Anderson

Urban Design Criteria: Lower Manhattan Landfill Richard Weinstein, Terry Williams, Richard Baiter, Jack Freeman, Leila Gilchrist, Susan Heller, Foon Chong— George Yee.

Wall Street Flower Show: Kenneth Halpern, Anne Wadsworth, Susan Jones

Work done in the Office of Midtown Planning and Development from 1969:

Clinton Park Housing: Bernhard Leitner, Wolfgang Quante, Doug Yi

Design Review: George Lawrence, Merrill Pasco, Stephen Quick, John Turnbull, Terry Williams

Fifth Avenue Special District: Jaquelin Robertson, William Bardel, Lauren Otis; Norman Marcus, Pares Bhattacharji; William Fain, Robert Ponte, Stephen Quick

Madison Avenue Mall: Consultants: ECOS Ltd.—Van Ginkel Associates; Jaquelin Robertson, William Bardel, Lauren Otis; Richard Basini, David Borden, Jeffrey Brosk, Robert Brugger, Mazie Cox, Jeffrey Ewing, William Fain, Kenneth Halpern, H. T. Kuo, Donald Miles, Caroline Tripp, David Vander

Queensboro Bridge Study: Ross Burckhardt, Michael Kirkland, Susan Myers, Peter Seidel

Times Square Special District: Stephen Quick, Kenneth Halpern; Robert Brugger, Robert Flahive, Theodore Howard, Michael Kirkland, H. T. Kuo, Brian Logie, Colin Stewart, David Vandor

West Midtown Project: Jaquelin Robertson, Lauren Otis, Wolfgang Quante: Alexander Caragonne, Jan Jon Han, Bernhard Leitner, Bonnie Marantz, Stephen Quick, Rumi Shroff, John Turnbull, Terry Williams

Illustration Credits

1 Photograph courtesy of the Empire State Building Company
3 From Le Corbusier, *Oeuvre Complete,* by permission of the publishers, Artemis Verlag
4, 5 From *Architecture: action and plan* by Peter Cook, reprinted by permission of the publishers, Reinhold/Studio Vista
6, 7 & 23 Photo by Bettina Cirone, used by permission of the City of New York
22, 23 Drawings used by permission of the City of New York
24 Photos by Bettina Cirone, used by permission of the City of New York
25, 26 Drawings used by permission of the City of New York
27 Drawing used by permission of John Portman and Associates
28, 29 Drawing used by permission of the City of New York
32 From the *Metropolis of Tomorrow,* by Hugh Ferriss
33 Jerry Spearman, used by permission of the City of New York
34 Photo and photomontages by Jerry Spearman and Douglas Collins, used by permission of the City of New York
35, 38 Drawings used by permission of the City of New York
39 Drawing used by permission of Norman Jaffe, photo by Bill Rothschild, used by permission
40 Drawing by Le Corbusier from Frederick Etchell's translation of *Towards a New Architecture,* John Rodker edition
44, 45, 46, 47 Drawings used by permission of the City of New York
49 Photo by Bettina Cirone, used by permission of the City of New York. Drawing by Tesla
51, 53, 54, 57 Drawings used by permission of the City of New York
57 Photo by permission of the City of New York
59–67 Drawings used by permission of the City of New York
69, 69, 80 Drawings by office of Giorgio Cavaglieri, used by permission of the City of New York
72 Drawing by Marcel Breuer and Associates
73 Model photographs by Jerry Spearman, used by permission of the City of New York, drawing used by permission of the City of New York

Index